PRAISE FOR *FORGED*

"Honest, authentic, and compassionate, T. C. Moore gives voice to the deep rifts that preclude people from belonging in the American church today. Moore draws from the wisdom of his own forged-family story to encourage hospitality and extend hope to readers. His storytelling paints a picture to help all understand the radical, countercultural welcome of Jesus."

—**Jenai Auman**, writer, artist, and author of *Othered*

"This is a deeply autobiographical book that beautifully illustrates the good news of Jesus Christ. It should be read alongside Howard Thurman's *Jesus and the Disinherited*. T. C. Moore's journey from an abusive childhood through drug abuse and gang membership to being a pastor could have been told as a stereotypical story of evangelical conversion. Instead, it is a powerful meditation on the meaning of Christian community, especially becoming siblings in the Spirit. Moore's passionate criticism of popular American religiosity and other abusive structures of American society is timely, but the true heart of the book is how God's grace forges misfits, outcasts, and disenfranchised into a family that is stronger than biology."

—**Craig D. Atwood**, professor of Moravian theology,
Moravian University School of Theology

"Rev. T. C. Moore's ability to reflect on the gospel as it relates to life is impressive and inspiring! His storytelling, biblical acumen, and love for people shine throughout the book. His is a perspective rooted in experience, and his own story, as it informs his ideas, is compelling. As a theologian and social ethicist, I highly recommend this book for pastors, seminary students, and lay people who are interested in challenging traditional Christian views of family and forging a new, gospel-centered reality."

—**Michelle Clifton**, PhD, director of prison education, Lewis University

"Wow! T. C. Moore has given us a gift by sharing his life—which includes jaw-dropping experiences along with a wealth of knowledge gained through his voracious appetite for reading. Yet *Forged* is more than a collection of stories and lessons about life; it is a prophetic call for followers of Jesus to live genuinely as siblings in the faith. *Forged* is also an invitation to all who have been beaten down, who wonder if they truly belong anywhere, or who feel as if no one cares about them, to know that there is such a thing as loving community. Read this book and give away copies because we all need the challenge and the encouragement that T. C. Moore offers us."

—**Dennis R. Edwards**, dean of North Park Theological Seminary and author of *Humility Illuminated*

"Through a captivating narrative, Moore illustrates the transformative power of an extravagant gift and its impact on one's sense of worthiness and belonging. The author weaves together themes of grace and covenant, revealing a deeper understanding of God's love and our purpose. *Forged* reminds us that grace is not mere charity; it forges a covenant family, empowering us to embrace our true potential."

—**Glen A. Guyton**, executive director,
Mennonite Church USA

"In *Forged*, T. C. Moore invites us to join him on a compelling journey, in a way that will resonate with readers' own struggles, hopes, and questions. Through memoir and scriptural reflections, Moore intertwines the threads of transformation, justice, belonging, and radical love, inviting readers to embark on a profound exploration of kinship in Christ that transcends social boundaries. This book will resonate with both doubters and disciples of Jesus, offering a transformative vision for community in Christ. I've known T. C. for about a decade now, and this is precisely the kind of gift I would expect him to put into the world. Read this book!"

—**Drew G. I. Hart**, professor of theology, Messiah University,
and author of *Who Will Be a Witness? Igniting Activism for
God's Justice, Love, and Deliverance*

"In *Forged*, Moore exposes our society's utopian notions of community and the brittle limitations of the nuclear family as gospel. Through riveting stories grounded in scriptures, a robust theology, and cultural humility, Moore beautifully depicts what Jesus intended all along: for the web of true kinship to tether us by the Spirit's generous invitation for all. For followers of Christ, this ever-forging family can compel us into new rhythms of life together, wading together through the waters of redemptive conflict with resilience, dismantling the walls of hostility formed by racism. *Forged* will awaken us to the potential of family all around us. Read this book with your community, both formed and newly forged, and never settle for a vision that is less than what God intended for the family."

—**Rev. José Humphreys III**, author of *Seeing Jesus in East Harlem* and *Ecosystems of Jubilee*

"The news media centers stories of abuse in churches today, but in T. C. Moore's *Forged* I found an oasis of good news. T. C. Moore's story of faith is a story of family—family not there, family failing to be what family is designed to be, discovering the kin(g)ship established by Jesus, and growing into pastoring churches into churches as families. In *Forged* we do not read an idealistic, cookie-cutter model of the church; instead, we see real people forging real relationships with real struggles, finding that a forged, kinship family is the context for human realities. *Forged* will challenge church leaders and stimulate seminary classrooms into thinking about what God wants churches to become—families."

—**Scot McKnight**, Julius R. Mantey Chair of New Testament, Northern Seminary, and author of *The Jesus Creed* and *A Church Called Tov*

"Following Jesus isn't just about getting into heaven but about being a part of a new kind of family. In a time when many Christians are concerned about what is happening to the family, T. C. Moore shares the many ways followers of Jesus are to be a part of a new kind of family that loves no matter what."

—**Mason Mennenga**, YouTuber and podcast
host of *A People's Theology*

"The view of family that many entertain does not fit the belonging central to the family of faith. T. C. Moore points out potential idolatries associated with the nuclear family and proposes an alternative vision of family forged in response to God's love. Using personal stories and cultural connections, Moore calls for the families of love we desperately need and desperately need to become."

—**Thomas Jay Oord**, director of Northwind
Theological Seminary's doctoral program
in Open and Relational Theology and the Center
for Open and Relational Theology, and author
of *Open and Relational Theology* and other books

"T. C. Moore has written an important book that is essential reading for the American church at this time. Moore engages in the prophetic practice of truth-telling, expressing theological truth to a broken ecclesial reality. The church needs to heed Moore's call for a more theological vision of family and the family of God. This book demonstrates the full positive possibility of pastoral theology, offering real-life stories, biblical reflection, and theological application for a necessary re-forming of our ecclesiology."

—**Soong-Chan Rah,** Robert Munger Professor of
Evangelism, Fuller Theological Seminary, and author
of *The Next Evangelicalism* and *Prophetic Lament*

"T. C. Moore writes with an exquisite blend of street cred, crisp wisdom, theological nerdiness, and heartfelt hope for the planet. In the best possible way, this book will expose your unexamined assumptions about what Jesus says (and doesn't say) that a family is supposed to be. Disguised as a page-turning, midlife memoir drawn from a stirring life story spanning New Orleans, Boston, Los Angeles, and the Twin Cities, *Forged* is a must-read for followers of Jesus living in post-pandemic times."

—**Rev. Dan Stringer,** team leader, InterVarsity
Grad & Faculty Ministries in Hawai'i, pastor of
Theological Formation, Wellspring Covenant Church

"T. C. Moore offers a compelling invitation to move beyond indifference to interdependence."

—**Dr. Jer Swigart**, cofounder and executive
director of Global Immersion and coauthor of
Mending the Divides: Creative Love in a Conflicted World

"*Forged* could not arrive at a more urgent time. Identity, belonging, and Christianity are concepts in flux, and Moore steps into the moment with a book that invites the reader to consider the promises and demands of Christ's kingdom in the twenty-first century. Moore eschews the individualism endemic to American Christianity and demonstrates why the new forged family of Christ's gospel matters. Insightful, piercing, and indispensable."

—**Joshua Tom**, associate professor of sociology,
Seattle Pacific University

"T. C. Moore's *Forged* left me moved by vulnerable storytelling and inspired by a Jesus-centered vision of a family bigger than biology. On each page the transformative power of the gospel is on full display—even as I admit to differing theologically in a few instances. One part prophetic provocateur and another part pastoral guide, T. C. Moore's *Forged* invites us to put its title into action: to *forge* a *family*, with Jesus, for the sake of the world!"

—**Kurt Willems**, lead pastor, Brentview Church, Calgary,
Alberta, and author of *Echoing Hope: How the Humanity
of Jesus Redeems Our Pain*

"*Forged* is the book we need for this moment. Never in history have humans had so many options for connection—and yet, belonging is at an all-time low. T. C. Moore weaves together his own story with the urgent questions of the moment: what does a chosen family look like in a world that celebrates individualism

FORGED

FORGED

FOLLOWING JESUS INTO A NEW KIND OF FAMILY

T. C. MOORE

Broadleaf Books
Minneapolis

Scripture quotations marked (NIV) are taken from the Holy Bible, New International Version®, NIV®. Copyright © 1973, 1978, 1984, 2011 by Biblica,
Inc.™ Used by permission of Zondervan. All rights reserved worldwide. www.
zondervan.com The "NIV" and "New International Version" are trademarks
registered in the United States Patent and Trademark Office by Biblica, Inc.™

Scripture quotations marked CEB are from the *Contemporary English Version.*
copyright (c) 1991, 1992, 1995 American Bible Society. Used by permission.

Scripture quotations marked NRSV are from the New Revised Standard
Version Bible, copyright © 1989 National Council of the Churches of Christ
in the United States of America. Used by permission. All rights reserved
worldwide

Library of Congress Control Number 2023019259 (print)

Cover image: Paper Texture - Shutterstock_1261857097, RF
Cover design: Faceout Studios / 1200

Print ISBN: 978-1-5064-8686-4
eBook ISBN: 978-1-5064-8687-1

For Terence J. Austria,
beloved mentor, shepherd, "uncle," and friend.

And for Tyson, T. J., and Trinity.

CONTENTS

1 | BLOWING UP THE NUCLEAR FAMILY

Then Jesus' mother and brothers arrived. Standing outside,
they sent someone in to call him. A crowd was sitting around him,
and they told him, "Your mother and brothers are outside looking
for you."
"Who are my mother and my brothers?" he asked.
Then he looked at those seated in a circle around him and said,
"Here are my mother and my brothers!
Whoever does God's will is my brother and sister and mother."

Mark 3:31–35[NIV]

WHEN FAMILY ISN'T

When I was eight, my mother put me out on the porch of our trailer home one night in the dead of winter. I woke up in my pajamas, covered in snow, with only my Batman pillow and a thin blanket. I beat on the door and yelled as loud as I could, but she wouldn't let me in. A neighbor eventually got involved and called protective services. This kicked off a whirlwind of events that included my mother's mental illness diagnosis, my placement in the foster care system, and years of abuse and neglect.

I have these foggy memories of sitting in a waiting room with my grandfather for what felt like an eternity until a doctor came out to tell me my mother was sick with something I later understood was schizophrenia. I also have cloudy memories of bouncing between foster homes for a time while my mother was committed. It was the first time I'd ever seen cable TV, so I remember watching a lot of Nickelodeon.

Being forcibly separated from my mother at such a young age was deeply painful. To this day, I can't watch that scene in the original animated version of *Dumbo* when his mother is taken from him and put in chains. It feels re-traumatizing. And when, eventually, my mother regained custody of me some time before I turned ten, she wasn't the same person I remembered. I now know how common it is for people to require medication to help stabilize their mental health, and there should be no shame in that. But as a child, I simply couldn't understand the changes my mother was undergoing. She just seemed like a zombie to me. She slept all the time and didn't have a personality. From then on, I had to learn how to fend for myself.

Maybe that's why she hated being on that medication and would routinely stop taking it. That would set off a period of manic behavior. Sometimes she'd just run up credit card debt on rent-to-own furniture and appliances we couldn't afford, or she'd give lavish donations to her favorite televangelist, Robert Tilton. Other times, her delusions would become violent, and she'd beat me mercilessly. Once, during a manic episode, I was so sure she was going to kill me, I couldn't sleep until I'd hidden all the knives in the house under my bed. Another of her delusions had her wander naked into the front yard. It seemed like all of her delusions were religious in some way. She was sometimes an angel, or sometimes I was. Often Carman, the cheesy (yet apparently sexy) Christian crooner, was coming to marry her.

As the only child of a schizophrenic single mother, my childhood was just about as far from the idyllic picture of a nuclear family as one can get. My closest relative was my grandfather, who genuinely loved me and was a kind and compassionate man. But most of my early memories were of him standing near the door, one hand on the doorknob, saying he was very busy and had to go. It seemed like he was always busy and always had to go somewhere else—anywhere but my house.

The rest of my extended family lived far away, either in extremely rural parts of our state or in other states altogether. They might as well have lived on the Moon. We were nothing alike, as though we were from different planets. While I was being beaten or neglected by my mom, no one seemed to care to ask how things were at home. While I was experimenting with drugs and alcohol and learning how to survive on my own in the city, they lived in the boonies, in a Norman Rockwell painting. While my friend group looked like the United Nations, they lived in all-White enclaves. While they were bemoaning the waning influence of fundamentalist Christianity in the broader American culture, I was learning how to sell dime bags and steal from department stores.

We may share some genetics, but it didn't seem like we were ever really family. It felt like they wanted nothing to do with me and my messy life. Like a lot of Americans, I had a picture in my head of a family with a mom, a dad, two point five kids, a minivan, and a golden retriever, but my life didn't measure up at all. Growing up without a father and not knowing how to talk about my experiences of abuse and neglect by my mother made me feel like an outcast, like I didn't belong in my own family.

THE NUCLEAR FAMILY WAS A LIE

A large part of the problem is the very concept of the nuclear family itself. Where did we even get the idea that the nuclear family was the ideal family? Who gets to decide these things? For eons humans lived in bands and tribes, interdependent groups of families, related not by blood but by a common life. After that, extended families, or clans, were the most common forms of family for millennia. It wasn't until the rise of Western individualism and capitalistic consumerism that the concepts of freedom and financial stability gave rise to the ideal of the nuclear family. And, even then, the ideal didn't last long, possibly only from around 1950 to 1965.

Furthermore, the so-called nuclear family only really benefited a select few: the relatively wealthy, White Americans, and men in particular. Only those with the financial means to sustain this independent lifestyle, and the social privilege to navigate it, thrived under this new model, which only served to widen inequality. Those who suffered were disproportionately women, people of color, and people with lower incomes. In the generations before, extended families provided a buffer against some of life's most turbulent disruptions. Extended families can pool their resources and cooperate to raise children. Extended families provided a connection to culture and heritage, history and tradition. The nuclear family wasn't built on traditional family values as people often think; it broke families apart, increased inequality, and traumatized children. "The period when the nuclear family flourished was not normal. It was a freakish historical moment when all of society conspired to obscure its essential fragility."[1]

Thankfully, a massive shift is taking place. The gravity of the 1950s' *Leave It to Beaver* model of family has lifted, and Americans are waking up to just how far from reality it always was. People are now longing for a village rather than an island. Instead of maintaining the facade of self-sufficiency, more and more adults and children today want to "live and grow under the loving gaze of a dozen pairs of eyes, and be caught, when they fall, by a dozen pairs of arms."[2] People are rediscovering the power of fictive kin and chosen families. As Maya Angelou once wrote,

> Family isn't always blood. It's the people in your life who want you in theirs; the ones who accept you for who you are. The ones who would do anything to see you smile & who love you no matter what.[3]

I know firsthand what Maya Angelou is talking about, because it's exactly what I've experienced since becoming a follower of

Jesus. Following Jesus ushered me into a new community and fundamentally transformed my understanding of kinship.

REIMAGINING KINSHIP

Kinship is typically thought of as the quality of sharing genetic relationships like parentage or siblingship. But kinship also extends to those who choose to become family through marriage. So already embedded within kinship are models of family through descent and family through affinity. And kinship means even more than these alone. Kinship is also the complex web of social relationships and narratives developed within a community and the identities they confer upon individuals and the collective.

Kinship matters because we do not make ourselves—we are formed by our relationships. We aren't abstract concepts, free-floating and disconnected from bodily life. Who we are is instead anchored to concrete experiences rooted in social contexts, with all their attendant customs, expectations, and philosophies. In his book, *Who God Says You Are*, Klyne Snodgrass calls attention to the many ways we derive our identity from our relational connections:

> You cannot be human by yourself. Your very existence depends on a community and always has. You cannot conceive of yourself in isolation. Rugged individualism— or any other kind—is an illusion. A community gives the language by which rugged individualism is understood, and other people tell you how to be an individual.

A community gives the language necessary for comprehending identity, and a community engages each of us in dialogue, telling us who we are and how we fit into a larger story.[4]

Following Jesus as his disciple invites a person to reimagine kinship, the story we are part of, and the identities that name our experiences. Jesus certainly isn't interested in preserving anything resembling a nuclear family. Jesus's call to discipleship is so radical that it even surprised his own mother and brothers.

When Jesus's family shows up in Mark chapter 3, they think he's gone insane. They arrive not with a mind to learn from him and become his disciples, but with the intent to "take charge of him." (Mark 3:21) Jesus cuts that off quick. He shows them they don't have a clue what's going on. They aren't the ones driving the story; he's the author and the main character.

> *Then Jesus' mother and brothers arrived. Standing outside, they sent someone in to call him. A crowd was sitting around him, and they told him, "Your mother and brothers are outside looking for you."*
>
> *"Who are my mother and my brothers?" he asked. Then he looked at those seated in a circle around him and said, "Here are my mother and my brothers! Whoever does God's will is my brother and sister and mother."* (Mark 3.31–35[NIV])

This new family Jesus speaks of supplants all the traditional identity markers of kinship with a new story that completes a very old story. Since the beginning, God has been forging a human family as a microcosm of God's broader dream for the whole world. Through this family God will bless all the families of the world (Genesis 12:2–3; Acts 3:25–26). Jesus is at the center of this new, multiethnic family God is forging (Galatians 3)—a family that defies conventional notions of family and disrupts traditional kinship networks. Willie James Jennings describes the process by which this new family is formed as a "mutual enfolding" in his groundbreaking book, *The Christian Imagination*:

> Imagine a people defined by their cultural difference yet who turn their histories and cultural logics toward a new determination, a new social performance of identity. In so doing, they enfold the old cultural logics and practices inside the new ones of others, and they enfold the cultural logics and practices of others inside their own. This mutual enfolding promises cultural continuity measured only by the desire of belonging. Thus the words and ways of one people join those of another, and another, each born anew in a community seeking to love and honor those in its midst.
>
> The new people formed in this space imagine the world differently, beyond the antagonistic vision of nations and toward the possibility of love and kinship.[5]

Jesus's call to discipleship disrupts our social categories of kinship that are rooted in fault lines drawn before we were born. Jesus calls us out of rivalry and conflict and into a society built on love. As pastor Melissa Florer-Bixler writes, this new society is made up of people with whom "we have no natural relation and from whom we can extract no economic benefit."[6] This new radical form of kinship centered on Jesus challenges our most fundamental loyalties and allegiances.

THE GOSPEL OF THE KIN(G)DOM

Today when Westerners, particularly Americans, hear the word "gospel," we've been conditioned to think first about ourselves. For us, the gospel has become virtually synonymous with something called the "plan of salvation," a way we can be rid of guilt for sin so we can go to heaven when we die. This distortion of the gospel can be traced back at least to the Reformation (if not further back to the high Middle Ages), when the Protestant pioneer Martin Luther asked, "How can I enter a right relationship with God?" Since then, Western Christians of all stripes have had a tendency to invert the message of gospel from one about God to one about me and my salvation, as if the sun revolved around the earth.[7] One of the keen insights of the late Christian philosopher Dallas Willard was that in the modern American imagination the gospel has been reduced to a "sin management system."[8] In this way of thinking about the gospel, Jesus becomes little more than a mechanism for getting us the results we're after, a convenient means to our desired ends. But far from a feel-good message that makes us feel less guilty, Jesus preached that the reign of God is like a sword that turns family members against one another (Matthew 10:34–36). Consider how drastic Jesus's responses are to those who said they wanted to be his disciple but had to first attend to their families:

> *[Jesus] said to another man, "Follow me."*
> *But he replied, "Lord, first let me go and bury my father."*
> *Jesus said to him, "Let the dead bury their own dead, but you go and proclaim the kingdom of God."*
> *Still another said, "I will follow you, Lord; but first let me go back and say goodbye to my family."*
> *Jesus replied, "No one who puts a hand to the plow and looks back is fit for service in the kingdom of God."* (Luke 9:59–62[NIV])

Jesus's gospel immediately clashed with the established norms of family in the ancient world. Whether Roman or Jewish, families were highly protective of their honor and status in society. An honor system underpinned the household model that was characterized by patriarchy and utilitarianism, even if sometimes tempered by benevolence. Relationships between husbands and wives, siblings, patrons, and slaves were all governed by an anxious protection of power and wealth. As New Testament scholar David DeSilva writes about the ancient Greco-Roman context, "Ancient authors see a close correspondence between the household and the state, such that the former is a kind of microcosm of the latter," pointing to both Aristotle and Philo. Families were often also businesses. Homes were even designed with this assumption in mind, with rooms that faced a street and served as a type of storefront shop.[9] Strong households were expected to be the foundation of the empire's wealth. The stability of the household family model was jeopardized by challenges to traditional notions of kinship. Therefore, the destabilizing of kinship networks posed a very real threat for the empire as a whole (Acts 17:6–7).

Nevertheless, the Jesus movement multiplied exponentially throughout the Roman Empire, due to its extraordinary love modeled by Jesus and empowered by his Spirit. By announcing his reign over all the powers that be, and defeating death itself through his death and resurrection, Jesus laid claim to the world and redefined human community. People from every tribe and tongue, clan and culture, are now enfolded into a new way of being human centered around him (Revelation 7:9). Jesus fulfills the covenant promise of blessing by God to Abraham by expanding the identity of God's people to include allegiant disciples from every ethnic group on earth.

Jesus's gospel demands our allegiance and breaks open our old notions of kinship. It opens up the world to healing and wholeness through the creation of a new human family, a new social order that is renewing the world (Matthew 19:28–30). But the denial of the social dimension of the gospel is as old as Western culture itself. And this denial not only has dire consequences for the church but also for the broader world. Christians who deny the social dimension of the gospel end up contributing to social injustices in the name of Jesus. When we place ourselves at the center of the gospel, rather than Jesus's kin(g)dom, our "gospel" reflects the Western philosophy of rugged individualism more than the others-centered, collective culture of the kin(g)dom of God. This creates a type of syncretism, a Westernized form of Christian faith that is no longer recognizable as the Jesus Way. This is what Soong-Chan Rah calls the "Western, white cultural captivity of the church" in his book *The Next Evangelicalism*:

> The American church, in taking its cues from Western, white culture, has placed at the center of its theology and ecclesiology the primacy of the individual. The cultural captivity of the church has meant that the church is more likely to reflect the individualism of Western philosophy than the value of community found in Scripture. The individualistic philosophy that has shaped Western society, and consequently shaped the American church, reduces Christian faith to a personal, private and individual faith.[10]

A syncretistic gospel that enshrines individualism and produces a privatized piety is a false gospel that blinds Westerners to humanity's interrelatedness, the systemic nature of sin, and how the reign of God is renewing the whole world. A private and individualistic faith precludes the need for social appropriation of the gospel. As Rah and Mark Charles succinctly state in their book, *Unsettling Truths*, about the ongoing dehumanizing legacy of the Doctrine of Discovery, "the captivity to individualism in the West leads many to reject the possibility of institutions and systems inflicting social harm that requires a social response."[11]

This failure to see the social dimension of the gospel was also one of the most poignant insights sociologists Michael O. Emerson and Christian Smith reveal in their landmark book, *Divided by Faith*. More than two decades ago they pointed out that White and Black Christians in America, who shared the same "evangelical" faith, nevertheless had very different views on race due to the inadequacy of the "religio-cultural tools" employed by White Christians to address racism in America. Emerson and Smith called these tools: 1. Accountable free-will individualism; 2. Relationalism; and 3. Anti-structuralism "(inability to perceive or unwillingness to accept social structural influences.)"[12] Christians who are held culturally captive by individualism develop a fatal flaw that prevents them from recognizing the way the Gospel subverts systemic injustices like racism. "Because [racism's] existence is not recognized, action is not taken to overcome it."[13]

If we fail to see the social dimension of the gospel, we not only forfeit our authority to speak truth to power, we also forfeit our calling to be agents of healing in the world. We can't be part of God's healing if we are too busy reproducing the virus. This was a central truth taught by the late Native American theologian Richard Twiss in his prophetic book *One Church, Many Tribes*. "As the family of God, we are being called to bring healing to these divisions among cultures and people groups and to demonstrate to the world a power and grace to walk with one another in true honor and respect, declaring that there is a better way—the Jesus Way."[14] The Jesus Way provides us with a new vision for societal healing. But by reducing the gospel to catchy slogans or a plan of salvation for individuals, a golden ticket to heaven, churches have walked away from the true gospel and have left a hurting world abandoned.

JESUS'S FAMILY SUBVERTS EMPIRE

The gospel boldly declares that God's new social order has invaded the old and is transforming it. Jesus is the rightful king who displaces all other rulers and disrupts every system of power that oppresses people. In Jesus, the powers of evil have been principally defeated through his life, his teachings, his signs, his advocacy for the poor and marginalized, his vicarious death, and his victorious resurrection. Jesus has principally defeated the forces which drive people apart, create the fear of scarcity, and breed sinful ignorance, hatred, and violence (Hebrews 2:14–15). This also means that all the claims of empires and emperors to bring peace and justice are exposed as lies. Like the so-called *Pax Romana* that was established through conquest, princes and presidents promise peace through violent means. Such peace is law and order for the poor, wealth and privilege for the rich. But the true king, the Jewish Messiah and Lord of all nations, establishes true *shalom* (wholeness, harmony, justice, and peace) for the whole world through the power of God's love and the Holy Spirit.

With the powers defeated in principle, together with all our diverse identities, those of us who are allegiant to King Jesus form one new human family united in Christ—a new way of being human community together. This new community isn't divided by gender or culture or ethnicity or race or orientation or class. This new community is united by the gospel that Jesus is Lord. His story has brought to a climax the story of Israel, the people of God, and points the way forward to new creation.

This is why theologian Ada María Isasi-Díaz proposes we appropriate the gospel in today's world with a more fitting metaphor: the *kin-dom* of God. She writes, "It is, then, in keeping with what Jesus/the Gospels' writers did to communicate a message (use 'kingdom' to refer to a world order different from the dominant one) for us today to use other metaphors that better communicate that message."[15] The metaphor of a "kingdom" was Jesus's way of describing a value system, way of being, and social order that emanated from God's life and love. However, in today's world, "kingdom" often connotes authoritarian and patriarchal structures rather than the relationships of mutuality and reciprocity Jesus modeled and commanded. Instead of a top-down order, Jesus taught humility and hospitality. Rather than dominance, Jesus modeled servanthood. The reign of God that Jesus preached was a new way of being human family:

> Kin-dom of God very much hinges on the way Jesus molded his disciples into his new kin. Kin-dom as metaphor can be valuable in helping to create a contemporary understanding of the world order that Jesus worked and died for. It values kinship without canonizing the patriarchal family. It moves from the elitist and authoritarian characteristics of kingdoms and empires and focuses instead on relationality and mutuality. It

highlights forgiveness and love as values characteristic of the new world order. Being a fictive kinship, it rejects exclusion and instead endorses inclusion of new members as a blessing [. . .] Kin-dom of God brings new understandings that strengthen the sense of mutuality, justice, and peace to Christian communities and to society at large.[16]

That's what this book is all about. And that is what my life is all about. For more than twenty years, I've had a front-row seat to God forging the kin(g)dom of God all over the United States—from the housing projects of New Orleans to dorm rooms at MIT, from tents on the streets of Skid Row to backyards in Hollywood. Not only have I seen it, I've become part of it. God is renewing all things, and it starts with following Jesus into a new kind of family.

2 | BLOOD IN, BLOOD OUT

About eight days after Jesus said this, he took Peter, John and James with him and went up onto a mountain to pray. As he was praying, the appearance of his face changed, and his clothes became as bright as a flash of lightning. Two men, Moses and Elijah, appeared in glorious splendor, talking with Jesus. They spoke about his departure, which he was about to bring to fulfillment at Jerusalem. Peter and his companions were very sleepy, but when they became fully awake, they saw his glory and the two men standing with him. As the men were leaving Jesus, Peter said to him, "Master, it is good for us to be here. Let us put up three shelters—one for you, one for Moses and one for Elijah."

(He did not know what he was saying.)

Luke 9:28–33^{NIV}

DESPERATE FOR FAMILY

"Full body or neck down?" The question wasn't a surprise at all because I knew I'd eventually have to decide and I'd thought about it a lot. If I chose "full body," it meant the beating would last three minutes. In those three minutes I could be punched anywhere, including directly in the face, but I could also fight back. That might seem like an advantage, but I imagined fighting back would make those jumping me in hit even harder. Fighting back could backfire. But if I chose "neck down," the beating would last only one minute instead of three. While I wouldn't be able to fight back, I also couldn't be hit in the face. *Which would you choose?* I chose "neck down." I really didn't want to get hit in the face.

At thirteen I was violently beaten into a gang by my closest friends at the time, from the neck down, for a minute that felt like an eternity. I'd seen others get jumped in, and I knew some who were seriously hurt in the process. Often, when people learn this about me, they ask me what could possibly have possessed me to submit myself to such a dangerous and barbaric ritual. The answer is simple. *Belonging. Brotherhood. Family.*

I was a teenager who'd never known the love of two parents, the bond forged between siblings, or even the care of extended family. It's way too easy for someone who was raised with all that privilege to judge young men or women who join gangs because they're desperate for family. If you've never been abused or neglected, abandoned and alone, then you don't know how attractive the promise from a gang of protection, purpose, and provision is.

"Family" is such a powerful concept that it can be easily used in manipulative and abusive ways. Unscrupulous people can wield the promise of a relationship that includes safety and love to control, exploit, and destroy others. It happens all too often. So, before we journey any further into what it means to forge family, we must first confront some of the realities of dysfunctional family. If we're going to forge family in a way that is healthy, it's important that we're able to recognize unhealthy ways of being family and the types of institutions, systems, and structures that produce them. But, first, we have to acknowledge that some of the reasons people are attracted to and remain in toxic families are perfectly understandable.

THE BRIGHT SIDE OF GANG LIFE

"I hear you're in college?" he said like a question. My "OG" could be very intimidating. He was from East St. Louis and had scars on his face from the spray of a shotgun blast. He was infamous for his deadliness, and I wasn't sure if I should admit to him I was a student, but I did anyway.

"I'm just taking a few community college classes," I said, trying to downplay it.

"Good," he said, "you should get an education. Everything you learn could be useful."

Believe it or not, the most encouragement I received to stay in school at sixteen was from a gang leader.

Looking back, I can clearly see all the toxicity that I was immersed in while I was gang-involved. But at the time, it was the closest thing to family I'd ever experienced. Not only was I welcomed into a brotherhood where I found identity and belonging, I was also given opportunities to show leadership, and my gifts and skills were put to use. Before we reflexively reject gang life as a corrupting influence, it's important that we acknowledge what it does well. That way, we can reproduce the positive aspects while rejecting the negative ones.

Gang life is principally about loyalty. Members forge a powerful bond precisely because membership is costly. A decision must be made: Are you in or are you out? Whatever can be said about gang members, they aren't wishy-washy—they're committed. Gang life also requires collaboration. The gang is on a mission, and every member joins in. This gives everyone a sense of purpose, direction, and meaning, even if the mission is illicit or destructive. Gang life also involves a common life, a rhythm of practices, a set of shared symbols and customs. This contributes to shared meaning, shared identity, a collectivism that incorporates the individual into the whole. On their own, each of these is a positive trait of close relationships, forged family. It's when these are combined with harmful and traumatizing elements that they become dangerous and unhealthy.

It's a powerful feeling to belong to something bigger than ourselves, to know that we're needed, wanted, and have a place. Shared symbols, shared rhythms of life, and shared practices all contribute to a sense of identity in which we can take pride. But for all the same reasons these are powerful, they also have the potential to be used against us. When belonging is leveraged to coerce, it becomes abusive. And unfortunately, this happens all too often in organizations where institutional reputation and financial sustainability are valued above the well-being of people.

BUILDING TABERNACLES, MISSING MIRACLES

Following the Jesus Way into forged family requires walking away from harmful cultures, organizational structures, and institutions. The Jesus Way is a movement, not a particular 501(c)3 organization. The Jesus Way is practiced among people who are caught up in the Spirit of God, and the Spirit moves wherever she pleases. The Jesus Way may lead you to forge family with others in the context of a particular local church, but it also may lead you to walk away from an institution that calls itself a church but is less concerned with forming a community of Jesus-disciples and more interested in building a brand or having a surplus in the annual budget.

The Gospel recounts an episode in the life of Jesus when he revealed his heavenly glory to a small group of his disciples on top of a mountain. We call this the Transfiguration, and many traditions commemorate this moment annually. Peter, one of those few who was invited, is often presented in the text as a sort of representative for the reader—making the mistakes we as readers and disciples often make. Right in the middle of this miracle, that even involved the appearances of Elijah and Moses, Peter blurts out, "Master, it is good for us to be here. Let us put up three shelters—one for you, one for Moses and one for Elijah" (Luke 9:33). Imagine losing the plot so spectacularly that instead of basking in an extraordinary moment shared by only two other people in human history, your mind wanders to thoughts of building construction. Luke frankly tells us, "(He did not know what he was saying.)" But today this is a standard occurrence. The construction and maintenance of structures and institutions, both figurative and literal, too often takes precedence over the miracle of forging family in the way of Jesus.

In fact, far too often the preservation of an institution is even prioritized before the safety and well-being of people— particularly women and children. Laura Barringer and her father, Scot McKnight, point this out in their book *A Church Called Tov*, that details the warning signs of toxic culture in churches.[1] They were a part of Willow Creek when its senior pastor, Bill Hybels, was accused of harassing and abusing multiple women. They witnessed firsthand how toxic church cultures develop, how they're maintained, and how they react when confronted. Toxic church cultures are often organized around a charismatic leader who exhibits narcissistic personality traits and surrounds themselves with admirers who are also enablers. For the narcissistic leader, control is paramount. That's why they often ensure that the structure of the church is unaccountable to any larger body. They may have a board, but board members are often hand-picked and can be easily dismissed if they push back against the pastor's wishes. This leads to an authoritarian type of leadership.

Toxic church cultures also motivate with fear. They may use their tradition's injunctions on what they consider sinful practices to regulate behavior, or they may use the fear of eternal damnation itself. But often they leverage the fear of being ostracized from the community. Fear can also be used to insulate the leadership from criticism. Maybe the pastor has cultivated a mystique of spiritual authority or giftedness that can't be questioned. Or maybe they are considered larger-than-life personalities, too important to be saddled by mundane concerns. This creates a fear of the leader, and admirers replicate this kind of fear-based leadership.

Whether a church culture is toxic is often revealed by how it handles confrontation. A healthy church culture will respond to its failures with confession and repentance. When accusations are made, it will want a thorough, independent investigation to be conducted to find the truth. By contrast, a toxic church culture will immediately flip into damage control and defensiveness, and spin false narratives against those who have made allegations or have valid criticisms. Toxicity can be seen in the prioritization of the institution over human beings.

Over the past two decades, I've unfortunately had more than a few experiences with toxic church cultures and have sensed God's Spirit urging me and my family to leave several. I've been a part of churches with narcissistic lead pastors who could never be challenged. And with my personality as a challenger, conflict was inevitable. I've also been a part of churches with leaders who have cultivated fear-based cultures using their spiritual gifts as weapons. They used prophecy manipulatively, what's been called "proph-a-lying." God seems to conveniently always want what they want and oppose their detractors. I was also on the staff of one church in which I discovered a pastor was defrauding a grant funder and potentially embezzling funds from the program I was leading. When I notified the senior pastor, he said, "You know he's my brother-in-law, right?"

Church institutions are susceptible to mission drift. They start out with a vision for spreading the gospel, and they end up circling the wagons. They start out wanting to heal people, and they end up inflicting harm. We can recognize toxicity when church becomes the brand, the bank account, and the building, rather than the people.

Nevertheless, church communities have also been some of the spaces where I've forged my closest family bonds. Not all churches are interested in packing out stadiums or even owning property. Some of the churches where I've connected the most deeply with others, felt most loved, affirmed, and equipped, have been the most informal communities. This is no accident. A community shows you its values by that in which it invests most. Owning a building isn't necessarily immoral for a church. But for what purpose? Is it to provide a space all week for the community to use? Or is it empty most of the time? Is it to set down roots in a particular neighborhood which the church feels called by God to invest in, support, and serve? Or is it a monument to the church's wealth arbitrarily located wherever is most convenient to commuters? Churches have the opportunity and the calling from God to be spaces where family is forged. But that requires focusing resources and energy on developing people and their relationships, rather than building an organizational structure that becomes bureaucratic. This disestablishment posture keeps the church true to its purpose of living as a witness to the love of God through relationships—the kin(g)dom of God.

FAMILY AND DIFFERENTIATION

Churches are far from the only institutions that can develop toxic cultures. Biological families themselves can cultivate patterns of hiding, silencing, and shaming that harm their own members. The 2021 Disney animated film *Encanto*, with its vibrant colors and beautiful music, reminded millions of its viewers of some of the ways families can develop a toxic culture. A deeply traumatic event in the life of Alma, the matriarch of the family Madrigal, was the catalyst for a miracle that produced a magical candle, a hidden village (*Encanto*), and a sentient house (*Casita*) for her family to live in. Since then, the members of the family Madrigal were all endowed with superhuman gifts by the magical candle, except for Mirabel, Alma's grand-daughter. Because of this, she felt treated differently and left out. When Mirabel later has a vision of *Casita* cracking apart and the miraculous candle flickering out, she embarks on a journey to save her family and uncovers a secret—that uncle Bruno was ostracized and exiled from the family due to the disruptive nature of his prophetic gift. He and the visions he shared have been locked away in the walls of the house. The song from the movie composed by Lin Manuel Miranda, "We Don't Talk About Bruno," easily became a hit and was played on repeat in homes with small children as much or more than was "Let It Go" from Disney's *Frozen*.

Encanto artfully illustrates how toxic cultures can develop in seemingly functional families. As Richard Rohr has famously said, "If we do not transform our pain, we will most assuredly transmit it."[2] The unexplored trauma Alma Madrigal suffered morphed into controlling pressure, secrecy, and shame. This led to Mirabel's marginalization and Bruno's oppression. If we're going to forge family that doesn't transmit our trauma, developing toxic cultures, we have to talk about both Mirabel and Bruno!

We will have to lead with vulnerable courage and confront diffi-cult truths. We will also have to learn how to resist cultural forces that threaten to crack the foundation of our *Casita*.

Differentiation is a necessary part of being a healthy family. We are connected to our families, and we love our families, but we are also individuals with our own unique gifts and dreams. Steve Cuss is the author of *Managing Leadership Anxiety* and hosts a podcast by the same name. He specializes in the intersection of Christian theology and what's called family systems theory, pioneered by Murray Bowen. He talks about differentiation in a way that I've found very helpful. Differentiation is the opposite of both indifference and enmeshment. While enmeshment is an unhealthy way that we lose our identities inside our families, indif-ference is an unhealthy way we find our identities completely apart from our families. A healthy sense of differentiation is hav-ing clarity around where we end and our families begin. When we're differentiated in a healthy way, we can be a non-anxious part of a family system.[3] Differentiation also facilitates empathy rather than stifling it. Without differentiation, we will either not recognize the needs of others (indifference) or not recognize the needs of others as different from our own needs (enmeshment). And neither of those facilitates empathy. Empathy entails the capacity to accurately recognize the needs of others in addition to having the desire to help.

Family is such an inclusive, expansive concept for me due to my positive experiences with forged family that I can sometimes lose sight of how the very concept of family can seem exclusion-ary. For many, when they think of family, they think "insider" as opposed to all "outsiders." A dear sister in my church community named Renee reminded me of this during a time of dialogue when I was teaching on forged family. She reminded me that in some families, the threat of being ostracized is wielded as a weapon of control. But healthy differentiation empowers us to overcome such threats.

Mirabel's gift wasn't a superpower like her cousins'. But she did have a powerful gift. She discovered the power of knowing who she is in relationship to her family with a healthy sense of differentiation. She was able to appreciate her uniqueness as an individual while avoiding the toxicity of individualism. And she was able to repair the cracks in *Casita*, a symbol of the family's unity, by uncovering the unprocessed trauma in her family system and working through it with empathy and resolve.

SUNDAY NIGHT DINNER

When I think about escaping toxicity and forging family, I think about a season when I was on the pastoral staff of a church that had a narcissistic lead pastor. He was the kind that no one could question and who had insulated himself from accountability. When we had conflict, he would berate me furiously in the privacy of his office because no one outside the circle of his victims would ever believe he had such a violent temper. When I suggested we have a third party present in our private meetings, he erupted with anger and began spreading the false narrative that I was insubordinate and disrespectful. (I've been called things like that nearly my entire life.) After many grueling attempts to work through our areas of conflict, including professional counseling, nothing seemed to work. In the end, he and his hand-picked board forced me to sign a non-disclosure agreement in exchange for silence about his abusiveness or I wouldn't receive severance that my family desperately needed. That experience gave me deep empathy for people who remain in abusive systems because I often felt pressure to absorb the abuse for the sake of my biological family and the mission of the church. I was tempted at times to lose myself and submit to the soul-crushing system. But I'm also incredibly stubborn, which may have been a saving grace. I'm grateful I was able to get out, but we were far from unscathed. To this day, my family still lives with the scars of that painful experience.

However, in the midst of all that pain, something beautiful happened: forged family. My family grew close with a couple in that church community who viewed their ministry as extending beyond Sunday mornings and the neighborhood where the church gathered for worship, to their own backyard on Sunday nights. Jason and Christa cultivated the practice of inviting anyone they met that week, along with friends and family members, to their home for Sunday night dinner. This gathering of misfits and strangers didn't have a formal order of service, but it was worshipful. There wasn't a sermon, but there was always stimulating dialogue on matters that often included spirituality and religion. There wasn't a traditional communion practice, but there was always a great meal. There wasn't an elaborate liturgy, but before we ate, we'd make a circle, hold hands, and sing the Doxology.[4] Jason would often say, "Any and all harmonies are welcome," to the great relief of anyone like me who feared singing *a cappella* within earshot of a neighbor. And I'll never forget when my oldest son, who'd been deeply discouraged in his own faith due to the abuse I suffered, said to me, "This feels more like church." I knew exactly what he meant, and I felt it too.

Following the Jesus Way into forged family involves attending to the many relational dynamics that contribute to a healthy family system while resisting the traits of toxicity. Forged families are fiercely loyal. We show up for one another. We sacrifice for one another. We form a collective identity. But we don't lose ourselves or become doormats. A healthy sense of differentiation protects us from either enmeshment or indifference. Forged families have a common life filled with rhythms, practices, symbols, and ways of marking time together. But forging family in the way of Jesus means the circle is ever expanding. We are constantly inviting more people into our forged family. Forged families offer one another ways to exercise our unique giftedness, to lead, to teach, to model righteousness for others. But forging family also means making room for growth, learning from making mistakes, and giving one another grace. We're all on a journey together.

Jason and Christa modeled what forging family in the way of Jesus looks like for me and my family when we were wounded and exiled from a toxic institution. The world needs more Jasons and Christas and more Sunday night dinners.

3 | SETTING THE LONELY IN FAMILIES

When Jesus saw his mother there, and the disciple whom he loved standing nearby, he said to her, "Woman, here is your son," and to the disciple,
"Here is your mother." From that time on, this disciple took her into his home.

John 19:26–27[NIV]

THE SPIRIT SET ME IN FAMILY

By 1999, the "family" that gang life promised was crumbling. Whatever loyalty there was evaporated when more money got involved, and fault lines quickly surfaced over trivial matters between members who were supposed to be brothers. I was beginning to see the same abusive and neglectful patterns in the gang as I had in my own relationship with my mother. And I was constantly walking on eggshells, trying not to become a victim of the same violence in which I was now complicit. Once, I was pulled aside and warned that another member might have to be "taken out to the country" to be gotten rid of. His crime? He seemed to be spending a little too much time with rival gang members. What if next time I'm the one who is thought of as disloyal? Gang life was the most stable part of my life, and it was falling apart.

That was when a childhood friend named Nate called out of the blue. He knew what my home life was like growing up, the deep poverty and abuse, and he knew how I'd struggled as a teen. We went way back to elementary school. When we were little kids, our parents forced us to attend the same charismatic church on Sunday mornings, where all the youth were crammed into a literal garage outside the main church building and across the parking lot. Nate and I sat in the back of "God's Garage" and refused to participate. Even as tweens, we were mostly focused on getting drunk and smoking weed, but we did like the brand-new gym the church built for us to play basketball.

When we both dropped out of high school at sixteen, we were sent to a type of last-chance boot camp for court-involved Illinois youth run by the National Guard called the ChalleNGe Program. Every day for six months, drill sergeants would wake us up at 5:15 and make us run in formation for miles followed by "PT" (physical training). After we both graduated with a GED, we went our separate ways. Nate didn't know what I was going through when he called that fateful day. He didn't know that in the short span of the previous few weeks, I'd had two separate traumatic experiences that had me soul-searching like never before. The first was in a McDonald's parking lot when shots were fired after a fight. In a flash I visualized my death and the resulting newspaper headlines and thought about how stupid a place and way to die it would be. "Teen killed in gang shooting at McDonalds" is not the way I wanted to be remembered. The second was a car crash. Driving after an ice storm in the Midwest is always perilous, but driving under the influence after an ice storm is just plain stupid. Not long before Nate called, I'd wrapped my car around a telephone pole, driving too fast and not wearing a seatbelt. Somehow I didn't fly through the windshield. In fact, I didn't have a scratch. When a police officer arrived on the scene, he couldn't believe I'd even been in the car. I knew something had to give. I felt like my life was racing toward death.

Nate's call came as I was searching, longing for a new life, but I still didn't recognize the sound of salvation. He called to tell me that he'd turned over a new leaf. He'd stopped smoking weed, started reading the Bible, and he was going to be baptized. "That's all well and good," I thought, "but what's that got to do with me?" He was calling to invite me to be a witness to his baptism.

"I want you to be there," he said. I figured he was talking about the charismatic church we'd attended as kids, but he wasn't. He wanted me to meet him at a Pentecostal church across town. I knew nothing about Pentecostalism besides the warnings I'd heard from my extended family (who were Baptists). "They swing from the chandeliers," they'd said. I was very suspicious, but reluctantly agreed.

I struck up a deal with him. "I don't want to talk to any church folks. I just want to get in and get out. I'll be in the back and I'll see you get dunked, but then I'm probably going to leave. We can meet up someplace else later," I said. He agreed. But I had no idea how that night would change my life.

I arrived late on purpose and tried my best not to attract any attention. I sat in the back and didn't make eye contact with anyone. This wasn't a Sunday morning, but the sanctuary was filled with people. A large baptismal tank sat in the front of the room, just before the steps to the stage, flanked by a few men in dress shirts and ties, looking like preachers. In the front pew I saw several people all wearing matching grey sweatsuits. They were obviously the people getting baptized, and based on the order they were going in, it looked like Nate would be last. "I'm gonna be here all night," I thought. After each person was baptized, the entire choir stood up and sang an upbeat song with the person's name in it. Something like: "Amanda, Amanda, Amanda's on fire. She don't need the devil, 'cause the devil is a liar!" Every time they sang their song I grew a little more restless and annoyed. I zoned out and started thinking about my own life. What was I going to do? I felt trapped and alone, scared and depressed. Was my gang involvement going to get me killed?

That's when the banal pattern of the evening was suddenly disrupted. The pastor standing at the front and directing the service interrupted the choir mid-song. He waved and motioned with his hands for them to stop singing and take a seat. Then he bowed his head like he was deep in concentration. The awkward pause felt like it lasted way longer than it must have, as the entire congregation waited for him to say something. When he finally broke the silence, he apologized for how bizarre what he was about to say was sure to sound, and assured everyone that this was not something he was particularly thrilled about saying. He reluctantly but boldly shared details about a person he sensed had recently survived some close encounters with death. He shared about how this person was feeling and why it was that this person was now here, tonight, in their midst. He spoke as if he was reading that person's thoughts, knowing their fears and hopes. Then his message for that person turned blunt and confrontational. The "good news" he shared was more like life-saving surgery than therapeutic comfort. He said that the person was barreling toward death and was living in a personal hell. But tonight they had the chance to be rescued. He concluded with, "If that's you, I want you to come down here right now," and settled in to wait.

In the back of that room my chest tightened as I was trying to hide my face from the preacher. The Spirit was stirring inside me, but I didn't know what to do. Internally, I made a bargain with God, "If you can rescue me," I thought, "you can have my life. But why would you even want it?"

It would probably make for a much better story if at that point I'd triumphantly marched down the center aisle. But the truth is I was still too intimidated by all the church people in the room. Somehow I mustered up enough guts to slink around the outside of the pews, down to the front next to where Nate was sitting. He was startled and didn't understand why I was suddenly sitting next to him.

"What are you doing up here?" He asked. I couldn't look him in the eye, because I'd begun to cry. So with my head down, I said, "I think he's talking about me." That changed his entire posture.

He got excited and said, "You've gotta go up there!" Before I knew what was going on, I was standing in front of the pastor, and he was telling me to get dressed in the nearby restroom and return to the front row.

Ironically, I was baptized before Nate that night. The pastor led me in vows as I sat in the tank, and for the most part I had no idea what I was doing. But I could feel the Spirit stirring in me—new life was becoming possible. When I emerged from the water a feeling of lightness came over me, like I'd been carrying a heavy load on my shoulders for many years but it had suddenly lifted. In my heart, I felt like clouds parted and a voice from heaven was saying to me, "You are my beloved son, in whom I'm well pleased." I suddenly knew I was God's child, a new creation, a beloved member of God's family.

As I struggled to gather my composure and dry myself off with the towel I'd been handed, I noticed within me a strange desire to visit my mother, tell her what had happened, and give her a hug. It felt like an alien had taken over my body and mind. Love replaced resentment in my heart for her, and I had nothing to do with it. My tongue also didn't seem to work right after that. I couldn't bring myself to utter many of the same words that just hours before had easily rolled off my tongue. They now felt like a bad taste in my mouth. Friends who saw me in the days immediately following did double-takes. They looked into my eyes and said "There's something different about you. You've changed."

Everything changed. My world was turned upside-down. Suddenly, the center of my identity had shifted because of the new family to which I now belonged. Men and women in that congregation embraced me with the love of Jesus. They became aunts and uncles, mothers and fathers, sisters and brothers. I'd never experienced anything like it before. These strangers became the family of God for me. They became physical, tangible representations of God's love. They put flesh on the gospel. Their smiles became the smiles of God; their jokes became the jokes of God; their hugs became the hugs of God; and through them God spoke to me.

GOD IS LOVE

God is a father to the fatherless, setting the lonely in families (Psalms 68:5–6). God was already a family—before anything else existed (John 17:24). God is love (1 John 4:8, 16). Love isn't just one attribute among many, but God's very essence. God isn't a solitary kind of love, some kind of unrequited love. God is love perfected, love complete and whole. This is one of the oldest ways followers of Jesus have thought about God. God's nature is essentially relational, for God is the One Who Loves, the Beloved, and shared Love itself. The "Father" loves the "Son" in the love of the "Holy Spirit."[1] The love that defines God, the love that is the very ground of all being, is a shared love, a movement of giving and receiving. As womanist theologian Karen Baker Fletcher writes in her book *Dancing with God:*

> God, who is a spirit, moves in the world in *perichoresis*—a type of sacred dance, within God's own nature. [. . .] This community, traditionally called God, is one Spirit in three

movements. [. . .] The word *dance* in this text refers to the dynamic, ongoing movement of God in creation as God continuously creates and recreates, making all things new. [. . .] God, Jesus and his followers have often said, is 'like the wind.' One cannot see the wind, but one experiences its movement in the world.[2]

When the divine Spirit, this movement of love, flows through creation, family is forged. Genesis says that the Spirit "hovered" or "brooded" over the unformed, primordial waters like a bird that alights on her young and birthed creation through the eternal Word. "And God said . . . and there was . . ." The Spirit called forth humanity from the dust of the earth. "God created humanity in God's own image, in the divine image God created them, male and female God created them." (Genesis 1:27[CEB]) Family flows from the divine life, the love that turns the world. God delights in family because family is at the heart of who God is and for which the universe was made. God is a loving community of persons who give and receive of themselves, the first family. Family is so important to God that God recreates family when families fall apart.

A FATHER TO THE FATHERLESS

"Where's your father at?" Years later, the pastor who'd listened to the Spirit, read my mail, and baptized me, saw me standing off by myself at a church picnic. He came over and asked me why my father wasn't there. With shame in my voice, I told him that I'd never actually met him. His face turned serious, and he looked me directly in the eyes and said, "T. C., there are no illegitimate children, only illegitimate parents." Those words echoed in my mind for years afterward. And I genuinely felt like God was healing me.

In those first few years after my baptism, I gravitated toward music that centered the theme of God as father. I also deliberately prayed to God as "Father," and many of my earliest devotional reflections were about the "Father heart of God." But it still felt like I had some unfinished business. So, at some point I began inquiring about my biological father. I asked my mother about him and gathered as much information as I could. Armed with some crucial data points, I did some Googling. It actually wasn't that difficult to find him. With just a few choice keywords, I had a work address and email. I emailed him a few times but never got a reply. Several years later, I was in San Diego for a conference and decided to write him a letter and drop it off at his office. The letter said that I was in town for a few days and included my phone number if he wanted to get together for a drink or a meal. When I arrived at his office, I didn't expect to be so quickly met by a coworker. When I told them who I was dropping off the letter for, they asked if I'd like them to call him. "He's probably just out for lunch," they said. I froze. It suddenly dawned on me that I could hear his voice for the first time, and I wasn't ready. I panicked and emphatically said no. I left the letter, and all week I waited for a call that never came. That was my last attempt to contact my biological father. To this day, I've still never met him. And yet, I don't feel deprived. Following Jesus has provided me with many male mentors who have become spiritual father figures. From their widely varied experiences and backgrounds, I've gained a wealth of insights and perspectives I could have never received from my biological father alone.

Terry Austria is one of those spiritual father figures. He's Filipino American and from the Chicago suburbs. He grew up nominally Catholic and moved to Urbana to study at the University of Illinois. He was headed for a career as a lawyer when God derailed his plans. Instead, he ended up helping to plant a campus church and entered into vocational ministry serving college students. Terry was one of the pastors who was there the night I was baptized. He may have even been the one who handed me the towel I used to dry off. Even though I was still only sixteen, I began attending the college student gatherings on campus because after completing a GED I was taking classes at a local community college.

The college student gatherings Terry led were unlike anything I'd ever experienced. They were both contemplative and intellectually stimulating. For the first time I began wrestling with the big questions of life, and Terry provided the space and freedom to explore them. He called that space "Excel," which sounds like it would be a place for business success coaching, but instead it was a laboratory for the Holy Spirit. In those gatherings I learned to listen for the "still, small voice" of the Spirit and muster the courage to speak out loud what I'd heard. They were also the place where I learned how to recover from failure, to fall and get back up again. Terry taught me how to read scripture, how to pray, and how to fast. Terry also taught me many invaluable character lessons. I like to say Terry changed my spiritual diapers.

I don't know how it happened, but I started calling him "Uncle Terry." It was just natural. He's family, but he's more than a brother. He's an elder, a role model, and someone who could call me out when I was wrong—and I was wrong a lot! He listened to me in a way no one else did. He genuinely cared for me and wanted to see me thrive. He's one of the first men in my life who not only saw my potential but was willing to help me achieve it. When I think of Psalms 68:5–6, "A father to the fatherless, a defender of widows, is God in his holy dwelling. God sets the lonely in families," I think of Terry. Meeting Terry when I did, and having him in my life at that crucial time, was like God hearing the deepest cry of my heart and meeting me through him.

JESUS-GIVEN AND ABBA-SENT

At one of Jesus's most desperate moments—as he was praying in the garden of Gethsemane before his arrest and crucifixion—he called out to God as "*Abba*" (Mark 14:36), which was an intimate expression for a father, something like "Dad." He was in deep anguish knowing what he would soon have to endure. But he knew he could turn to his Father. This example is preserved in the Gospel to reveal the kind of relationship we, too, can have with God. The apostle Paul uses the same word in one of the earliest Christian writings, the letter to the Galatians. "Because you are sons and daughters, God sent the Spirit of his Son into our hearts, crying, 'Abba, Father!' Therefore, you are no longer a slave but a son or daughter, and if you are his child, then you are also an heir through God" (Galatians 4:6–7[CEB]). This paints a picture of the liberating Spirit of God freeing us from bondage and adopting us into the very family of God, even making us fellow heirs with Christ of God's promised inheritance (Romans 8.15). The Spirit cries out from within us to God with that very same familial language Jesus used. And this cry is answered by God, by drawing us into united community with spiritual siblings. As Michael Reeves writes in *Delighting in the Trinity*, "Together we cry 'Abba' and begin to know each other as brothers and sisters. For the new humanity is a new family; it is the spreading family of the Father."[3]

The Gospel of John recounts something that happened in the final moments before Jesus died on the cross. Jesus's mother was there, in agony, seeing her son being led to his death. But someone was with her, someone John calls the "disciple whom he loved." I like to think this was John's way of referring to himself with both pride and humility. But regardless of who it was, this person was part of Jesus's spiritual family. So, what did Jesus do? He entrusted the care of his mother into this person's hands. Jesus, while being led to his own brutal death, was thinking about what's best for his mother. What was best for her was to be cared for by his spiritual brother, a beloved disciple. Jesus set his own mother in family, in his spiritual family.

Jesus said he only does what he sees the Father doing (John 5:19). And what the Father is doing is drawing people into the family of God through the Holy Spirit. That's why when Jesus appeared to his disciples after the resurrection, he said, "Peace be with you! As the Father has sent me, I am sending you" (John 20:21[NIV]). Then he breathed the Holy Spirit onto them to symbolize their empowerment and commissioning as his ambassadors. Our mission is now to extend the family of God in the power of the Spirit. "As the Father has loved me, so have I loved you" (John 15:9[NIV]).

Jesus's family are those who mentor a young person who has never had a father, never had a sister, and never known the loving embrace of a family that wants to see them become the person God created them to be. Jesus's family is a place of belonging. Jesus's family are those who seek out and welcome in those who've been stigmatized, marginalized, and ostracized by society—those who love people regardless of what poses a challenge to their care. Jesus's family are those who surround the hurting, the grieving, the recovering, the addicted, the mourning, and the brokenhearted with an unconditioned love that transcends comprehension. Jesus's family are those who are willing to be ridiculed and mocked, slandered and snubbed, reviled and rejected to serve the ones whom Jesus loves. They are those who visit prisoners, touch lepers, and wash the feet of the unhoused. Family is a matter of justice. God provides family to those for whom family has been denied. God sets right the social conditions that unjustly disadvantage the family-less.

Jesus's disciples are still *Abba*-sent. You and I are enlisted in this movement of the liberating Spirit to become the family into which God is setting the lonely. This family-forging ministry of the liberating Spirit is conferred upon you and me even now. When God sets the lonely in families, it looks like spiritual mothers and fathers, aunts and uncles, adopting a teen as their own and making them feel loved. When God sets the lonely in families, we're given to one another the way God gave me Terry and Terry gave himself to me. We're given to one another to listen, to encourage, to model accountability, to provide a safe place to fall and a helping hand to get up again. That's how family is forged. All around us are people in need of a family to surround them with the kind of support I received. The Spirit sees them and hears the cry of their hearts. *Abba* God is forging a family and setting the lonely in it. And if we want to join this kind of family building alongside God, it's vital that we learn how to share our very lives with one another.

4 | SHARING OUR LIVES

He appointed twelve that they might be with him
and that he might send them out to preach.

Mark 3:14^{NIV}

UNCLE TERRY

Before I'd even finished drying off from my baptism, members of
that Pentecostal congregation had already begun welcoming me
to the family of God. It was very touching, but I also didn't have
a clue what to do next. After the experience of feeling like a
weight was lifted off my shoulders, I was walking on air. The
only thing that kept me from floating off into space were the
many questions this experience now raised. *What now? How do I
live this new life?* While questions were still swirling around in my
head, Terry introduced himself to me. The timing couldn't have
been better because what I needed wasn't a rulebook to follow;
I needed the kind of resourcing that can only come from a real,
flesh-and-blood person.

Terry exemplified masculinity and spirituality in a lot of ways
that opposed my presuppositions, and he was unapologetic about

it. I think he revels a little in defying stereotypes and making people think twice. He challenged my presumptions about what it means to be a follower of Jesus, showing both his human limitations but also offering an inspirational example to follow. For instance, Terry was unmarried and lived out his singleness with integrity. He wasn't resistant to dating or marriage at all, it just wasn't his top priority. This disabused me very early on of some toxic notions about family values, especially the kind that idolize marriage. He also modeled appreciation for expertise, scholarship, and the complementarity of faith and reason or science. This gave me permission to ask difficult questions and seek the truth wherever it may lead. He also wasn't ashamed to express emotion, to show sensitivity, but also had a quiet strength. He modeled a confident yet humble faith—a passionate faith that nevertheless rejects dogmatism.

Terry opened up his life to me and allowed me to see him not just as a pastor but as a human being. He let me into his world in a very vulnerable way by showing me that following the Jesus Way was possible even for people with real challenges in life. Even though he manages depression and anxiety and can be quite cynical at times, he is also incredibly confident and compassionate, and is a more than capable teacher. His courageous vulnerability instilled faith and hope in me that I continue to draw from to this day. Terry understands something that many Christians lose sight of: that the gospel incarnates itself through the lives of real human beings, and that authentic relationships are the foundation of a healing process that produces resilience.

RETHINKING RESILIENCE

Back then I didn't know any of what I do now about trauma. At that time, I didn't know how the abuse and neglect I'd suffered as a child, or the violent lifestyle I'd led, was traumatizing. Today, we have a lot more research and resources on trauma, but we still have a lot to learn about *resilience*. Much of the Western world still thinks of resilience primarily in individualistic terms. We tend to think that resilience is a matter of inner psychological strength or resolve. But what if we took another look at resilience, asking different questions?

A study published in 2017 measured resilience among Syrian refugee children. Researchers surveyed more than 600 youth affected by that war, but instead of asking them about their trauma, they asked them what resilience meant for them. The children's answers were revealing. For some, resilience meant being able to make new friends. For others it meant being able to adapt to their new home. "The young people said that resilience came from their ability to integrate into their new communities, to go to school and to work toward their dreams and ambitions." This ability isn't primarily an innate trait that some possess and others do not. It's facilitated by the resources and access the young people are provided. One of the researchers who developed the survey told a reporter, "If we find that a child's resilience is low, we can then explore that child's community and their surroundings more in depth, to find out why exactly."[1] The study concluded that the resilience of the refugee youth was a collective and social strength, something that is derived from friendships and community.

Consider how this approach defies Western assumptions. Rather than expecting traumatized persons to pull themselves up by their proverbial bootstraps (a saying that originally meant to do something that's impossible), this study suggests that resilience is strength and skills that can be provided by a caring and intentional community. Perhaps we've been victim-blaming all this time. Perhaps we should accept our collective responsibility to support those who've been traumatized rather than leaving their healing entirely up to themselves. Human beings deserve to live and aspire toward their ambitions. When a flower in a garden isn't blooming, we examine the environment first. We don't assume there's something deficient about the plant. Is the flower getting the light and nutrients it needs to thrive? Is this the right soil?

I didn't dig down deep and discover some hidden assets within my own psyche that enabled me to move beyond my traumatic childhood. No, it was quite the opposite. A loving community surrounded me, with all my faults, and provided a safe place for me to learn and grow. Caring adults viewed me as someone worthy of support, someone who they were now related to, and made space for me among them. When I needed to learn how to earn money legally, a deacon set me up with my first desk job, making far more than minimum wage. When I needed help navigating complex social systems, "aunties" and "uncles" held my hand as I filled out applications and filed paperwork. Forged family is a healing balm for traumatized people, a vital source of resilience. This is what Jesus was doing when he began to call to himself a community of disciples.

BEING *WITH* JESUS

Before Jesus's disciples were ever sent out to preach the kin(g)dom of God, they first had to spend time with him, learning from him. They needed to be in Jesus's presence, not only absorbing his words but also observing his actions. The disciples walked from place to place with Jesus, they set up camp, they ate meals, and occasionally Jesus would take off to be alone with the Father in prayer. They learned his rhythms and spiritual disciplines. This is why he chose them: to be *with* him first. Only through this close, personal relationship could the kin(g)dom of God be formed. This is the pattern of forging family we see all throughout the New Testament, including in the life of Paul.

After his Damascus Road experience with the risen Christ, it's fair to say Paul's (also known as Saul of Tarsus) trajectory in life was significantly redirected. He went from someone who was so vehemently convinced that Jesus and his followers were a threat to God's reign that he violently persecuted them (including approving of their executions by stoning, Acts 7:54–8:1), to someone who dedicated his life to planting Jesus communities all throughout the Roman world—often at great personal risk. He went from someone bent on imprisoning people for following Jesus as the Messiah to someone willing to serve Jesus-disciples to his dying breath.

In the first half of the first century Paul wrote to the Jesus community in the city of Thessalonica to encourage their faith. In the letter, he recounts how he shared the gospel with them—not a self-centered gospel nor a gospel slogan, but an *embodied* gospel.

He writes, "Just as a nursing mother cares for her children, so we cared for you. Because we loved you so much, we were delighted to share with you not only the gospel of God but our lives as well" (1 Thessalonians 2:7b–8[NIV]). Paul knew that the gospel couldn't only be shared with proclamation, it had to be demonstrated through his very life. He learned this from Jesus. Paul also knew that this type of life-sharing was like that of a mother who shares of her own body to nurture a child. Paul's use of a maternal metaphor here should not be easily brushed aside nor overlooked. Paul's identification of his own ministry in this maternal metaphor subverts stereotypes not only about what leadership looks like, but also about Paul's own view toward women.

The Jesus Way is an incarnational way of life, meaning it's embodied, showing up through everyday practices and the sharing of ourselves with others. Jesus made disciples not by downloading knowledge to their brains but by inviting them to walk with him, learn from him, imitate him, and take upon themselves his way of life. In the process, disciples became more than that—they became friends. Jesus said, "I no longer call you servants, because a servant does not know his master's business. Instead, I have called you friends, for everything that I learned from my Father I have made known to you" (John 15:15[NIV]). The movement Jesus birthed creates intimacy between people groups and forges new bonds of friendship that change the character of our lives. Building this kind of friendship sometimes just takes an invitation to a meal and the sharing of your stories with one another. Other times, it may require a bit more structure.

THE INTERNSHIP

To this day, I'm convinced Terry made up his internship program just to share his life with young adults he sensed God was calling him to invest in. My first time visiting the gathering he led for college students, he put me to work swapping out transparencies on the overhead projector during the musical worship. (I'm dating myself here.) But it was more than just busy work; it made me feel not only welcomed but needed. Not long after, he invited me to become an intern with him and the college ministry. I'd never had an internship before, and I wasn't too sure what one was. He said that I'd be serving around the church and helping to coordinate gatherings. I was way out of my depth, but I nevertheless agreed to take on this new role. It helped that I'd gotten to know others who were his interns in the past or were also current interns. I wasn't alone.

But, truth be told, I think Terry made it all up so that I could *walk* with him, *learn from* him, and *imitate* him. I think this was his way of creating a structure for discipleship, and it worked. I spent a lot of time praying with Terry. I also spent a lot of time praying by myself. He taught me how to pray, and I had a lot of questions. He taught me how to listen for the voice of the Holy Spirit and how to discern God's peace even when the decisions I had to make were difficult. He also taught me how to play a card game called Rook. (It seemed like Pentecostals frowned upon other kinds of card games, but not this one.) We laughed a lot, and we had fun. I also felt completely safe asking him questions about faith, life, and the Bible. Even a few times when I thought

I had it all figured out and would propose my sweeping new theological discoveries or theories, he was so patient with me. I once announced to him that I'd figured out the Trinity. Instead of calling out my obvious presumptuousness, he entertained my nearly incoherent ramblings with a combination of intrigue and bemusement. But that doesn't mean he didn't sometimes hold my feet to the fire. At some point in the internship, Terry discerned that my ego had gotten inflated and that I needed some tough love. He called me once at work and confronted me about the arrogant way I'd addressed a young woman who was Terry's close friend. I was undone. Like a father discipling his son, Terry shared not only the gospel with me but also his own life as well.

INVESTING IN LIVES

One night at Excel, Terry announced that he'd be starting a new teaching series for the next several weeks called "Investing in Lives." This series would explore what it means to be disciples of Jesus and to make disciples of Jesus. But rather than teaching discrete evangelism techniques, like how to use the "Four Spiritual Laws" with someone you meet out in the community, this series would be about how we become spiritual family for one another, extending our lives to one other. He shared a part of his story that I hadn't heard up to that point. While Terry was a student at the University of Illinois, he'd lost touch with his faith and felt adrift, not sure where his life was headed—other than to law school eventually and to earning as much money as possible. While he was still a student, he met a Pentecostal pastor named

Gary Grogan who began to meet with him and share his life with Terry. This began a spiritual transformation in Terry's life that shifted his trajectory from pursuing a career as a lawyer to pursuing a life of pastoral ministry.

While Terry was still speaking, in my mind's eye I saw a picture of a chain, and each link in the chain was someone who opened up their heart and shared their life with another person stretching back generation upon generation. I envisioned someone sharing their life with Gary, a bond through which Gary's life had been transformed by Jesus. Then Gary sharing his life with Terry, which led to Terry's life being transformed by Jesus. And now Terry was sharing his life with me, and my life was being transformed by Jesus. It dawned on me all in an instant what my purpose in life was. I wanted to be the next link in that chain. I wanted to devote myself to sharing my life with others so that Jesus could transform their lives. I remember trying to tell Terry all this less than coherently through tears later that night. I vowed to be the next link in that chain.

This only intensified Terry's internship for me. He began giving me more and more responsibility and debriefing my mistakes (which were plentiful). He appointed me an evangelism coordinator and put me in charge of leading young adults my own age and older than me. It was a steep learning curve, but he was always there supervising my fledgling attempts at leadership. He even gave me my first preaching opportunity while I was still seventeen. Twenty minutes before Excel was due to start, Terry unceremoniously informed me that I would be the night's speaker. I confess, I panicked. I even remember leaving the building, looking for a way to escape. But Terry found me and talked me back inside. He said, "The key to preaching is sharing from your own life. What is God doing in your life right now? Just talk about that." Terry's philosophy of preaching had a lot in common with his philosophy of discipleship—inviting others into your life. That night I shared from 1 Corinthians chapter 9: Paul's analogy of the life of faith in Jesus being like a race that one trains for. "Do you not know that in a race all the runners run, but only one gets the prize? Run in such a way as to get the prize. Everyone who competes in the games goes into strict training. They do it to get a crown that will not last, but we do it to get a crown that will last forever" (1 Corinthians 9:24–25[NIV]). I told the group about how it was beginning to dawn on me that if I'm going to finish this race, I needed to begin to cultivate practices that would sustain me for the long haul. The life of faith is more of a marathon than a sprint. There was nothing particularly profound about what I shared that night. I hadn't been to Bible college or seminary. I hadn't done any focused research or advanced exegesis. But what I had done is open up my life to others with the same kind of courageous vulnerability that I'd seen Terry model for me. With Terry's encouragement and support, I was able to step into a role that made me more fully who I am meant to be.

Too often, we've expected traumatized people to reach down deep and discover resilience in themselves, effectively making them responsible for their own healing, and simultaneously letting ourselves off the hook. We've said to the flower, "why aren't you blooming?" without tending to the garden in which they are planted. Opening our hearts and sharing our lives is a crucial part of the healing journey. Jesus created a movement of family-forging, resilience-instilling, healing. You and I are invited into that movement of the Spirit to share not only the gospel but our own lives as well. When we do, we make space for Jesus to transform lives and to make strangers into family. This family-extending, space-making movement is the gift of God—God's grace. But that doesn't mean sharing our lives with others will always be easy. Sometimes there will be conflict even between spiritual siblings. And when there is conflict we will need a framework for healthy confrontation, accountability, forgiveness, and reconciliation so that conflict can forge family rather than fracture it.

5 | TRANSFORMING CONFLICT

If your brother or sister sins against you, go and point out the fault when the two of you are alone. If you are listened to, you have regained that one. But if you are not listened to, take one or two others along with you, so that every word may be confirmed by the evidence of two or three witnesses. If that person refuses to listen to them, tell it to the church, and if the offender refuses to listen even to the church, let such a one be to you as a gentile and a tax collector.

Matthew 18:15–17[NRSV]

WE'RE IN THIS FOR THE LONG-HAUL

"Hey, T. C., would you put the seats back into the church van? They're in the gym," the youth pastor, Rob King, asked from his office. Rob was a clean-cut White guy who looked ten years younger than his age and like he'd just stepped out of a GAP ad. He could be a little goofy at times, especially during those ridiculous youth group games like "Chubby Bunny" (where the kids race to see who can stick the most marshmallows in their mouths and still talk). But most of the time he was intense like a coach who hated losing.

It was a Wednesday afternoon at the height of the summer, hours before youth group was due to start. I was also in the middle of my pastoral internship at the Pentecostal church where I was baptized and first became a follower of Jesus. Even though I was interning for the college ministry, I also helped out with the youth ministry. And, truth be told, I was still high school age, so it made sense.

What Rob was asking me to do was single-handedly lift those enormous bench seats that slot into the floor of a 15-passenger van, carry them out of the gymnasium to the church parking lot, and reinstall them. They had probably been removed to haul something too large to fit with the seats in place. It was close to 90° outside, and I wasn't happy to be asked to do this physically demanding task on such a scorching day, so I rushed it. I propped open the double doors of the gymnasium, so I could easily carry the seats through by myself. Several minutes later, after nearly breaking my back, the seats were installed, and I could get on with my day. Hours passed. I had other things to do, so I'd moved on. Then, suddenly, Rob loudly called me to his office, where he proceeded to chew me out.

"Do you realize you left the gym doors open?" He asked angrily.

"No, I must have forgotten to close them," I said, only just then realizing how obvious that statement was.

"Well, the air-conditioning has been running all day to cool off the gym for youth group tonight, and now the gym is boiling hot again because you left the doors open!" He was a little red in the face by this point. "Now, there's not enough time now to cool down the gym!" He yelled.

I started to feel defensive. Who does this guy think he is? I was doing him a favor. I wasn't being paid. I didn't have to carry those heavy seats all by myself. And I didn't appreciate being yelled at. So, I stormed out of his office and slammed the door. But, before I could get down the hall, he'd caught up to me and grabbed my arm. At this point, I could feel my body tense up like we were about to fight. I hadn't been a Christian long enough not to punch this guy in the face. But before I could swing on him, he said something to me that stopped me in my tracks, something I think about almost every time I have conflict.

He said, "T. C., I'm sorry I yelled at you. But we still need to work through this. In your old life, when you had conflict, you either handled it with violence or you cut those people out of your life. But we're family now; we're in this for the long haul. So, please come back to my office and talk with me."

What struck me so profoundly and has stayed with me ever since, is that something *had* shifted. I *was* a different person now. I *was* no longer satisfied with broken relationships or unresolved conflict. Even though I'd stormed out of his office, that's not who I wanted to be anymore. I knew he was my brother, and I was committed to this new family into which I'd been added.

IRON SHARPENS IRON

Why is it that we can have our most passionate conflict with family? Doesn't that seem somewhat counterintuitive? Shouldn't family be the people we get along with best? It might seem so. But, we've also learned through experience that the opposite of love isn't passionate conflict, it's indifference. The reason why we often have passionate conflict with family is because we love them so passionately. Love raises the stakes.

However, not all conflict is the same. Some conflict is very harmful. Conflict can be traumatizing—particularly when someone in the conflict is abusive. Other conflict is the result of being different and the process of differentiation (which we discussed in Chapter 2). This type of conflict—not the toxic, traumatizing kind, but the kind that comes from difference and differentiation—is part of the process of becoming family. It's this kind of conflict that is "iron sharpening iron" (Proverbs 27:17). We are refined in this kind of conflict, tempered like steel. This is precisely how family is "forged."

In Matthew 18, Jesus says,

> *If your brother or sister sins, go and point out their fault, just between the two of you. If they listen to you, you have won them over. But if they will not listen, take one or two others along, so that "every matter may be established by the testimony of two or three witnesses." If they still refuse to listen, tell it to the church; and if they refuse to listen even to the church, treat them as you would a pagan or a tax collector.* (Matthew 18: 15-17^NRSV)

There's much to unpack in Jesus's most succinct guide to conflict resolution. But before we dive too deeply into it, can we just acknowledge something that may be so obvious we often overlook it: Spiritual siblings sin against one another. Jesus takes this for granted. This is inevitable. Why? Because we aren't yet fully the people we will one day be, when we are perfected in God's love. In the meantime, we're learning and growing, and we'll make mistakes. When this happens, Jesus outlines a framework for reconciliation.

Second, it should also be said that this passage isn't about abuse or oppression. Jesus is not sending abused people back to reconcile with their abusers. Nor is Jesus teaching oppressed people to reconcile with their oppressors. Jesus is clear that this is sin between spiritual siblings—that means they're united in allegiance to Jesus and in equality as children of God. I'll say more about conflict that involves abuse and oppression later.

With those two notes made, let's examine this passage a little closer. The first step in Jesus's framework is direct, personal communication. And just like that, we've already hit a snag, haven't we? So many of us struggle with being direct. Wouldn't we just rather stuff our feelings down deep, never to be seen or heard? Wouldn't we rather just pretend nothing happened? Wouldn't we rather just avoid that person from now on? Of course. Jesus's first step is already challenging, maybe even especially for those of us who have been culturally conditioned to be passive aggressive. In case you're unaware, what they call "Minnesota nice" isn't actually nice.

This is one of those many times where we desperately need the Holy Spirit. One of my core values is a conscious dependence on the Holy Spirit. So when I'm wrestling with conflict like this, I'm praying and listening for the voice of the Spirit. I'm also asking the Spirit for courage, wisdom, and the actual words to say. Jesus believes so strongly in the power and presence of God's Spirit that he tells his disciples the Spirit will give them words to say when they are placed in circumstances which call for courage and direct communication (cf. Matthew 10:19–20). That sounds great, but it presumes that we're going to be obedient and allow the Spirit to speak through us, which is no easy feat either. I've had many of both experiences. On some occasions, I've been open enough to let God speak through me, and at other times I've failed. I've also been fearful, self-conscious, and disobedient. This first step is one of those areas of our discipleship that takes practice. We may never perfectly master it, and there's grace as we grow. But we're called to continually submit our whole selves to God, over and over. This entails receiving courage from the Spirit to be direct with spiritual siblings, letting God speak through us.

There's an important promise here that I don't want us to miss. Jesus says that if our spiritual sibling receives this confrontation and repents, we have "won" them. The verb there could be rendered either "won" or "gained." This type of "winning" isn't about being better or more righteous than the other person. The other person hasn't "lost"; we've both won. This person is already a spiritual sibling, but there's something about this process that strengthens our bond. We've learned more about one another. We've let them see a different side of us, and we've seen a different side of them. As a result of working through this conflict, we're closer now, more like family.

I know the truth of what Jesus is talking about here from a lot of experience. Over the years, I've been called on by God to do some direct communicating, confronting some siblings in Christ. It hasn't always been received well—we'll get to that later. But, when it has been received, those relationships are strengthened.

I've also been on the receiving end and have "gained" spiritual siblings who are some of my closest forged family to this day. I think this is part of what the proverb means when it says, "iron sharpens iron." Sure, we can sharpen one another merely by sharing ourselves with one another, our gifts, our experiences, our insights. And we are made better because of these things. But I also think we are sharpened when spiritual siblings have confronted us in love and helped us to see our areas of weakness and gaps in understanding.

I'll say this too: it's not always the more mature person who's doing the confronting. We're also sharpened by the grace *we* are shown when someone we confront is better at receiving correction than we are at giving it. And, honestly, many siblings in Christ do this confronting part badly. We can do it with pride in our hearts, misplaced anger, and harsh rhetoric. So, just know that we need the Spirit's help not only in gaining the courage to confront but also the grace to confront with love.

This leads me to another point about this first step. Before we go directly to our spiritual sibling with their sin, it's important that we take some time to reflect on the conflict. In his commentary on Matthew, N. T. Wright suggests: "The other person may well respond with a counter-accusation, and there may be truth in it which you need to recognize—though it certainly isn't always the case that both sides are equally to blame"[1] In this first step, it's important to acknowledge any place where you may also have fault. Often we sin against one another. But, as Wright wisely acknowledges, this isn't always the case. Sometimes one "side" is simply at fault and needs to repent.

STEP TWO

Now comes what to do when this first step fails. Jesus says that in
the event that a spiritual sibling does not respond favorably to our
direct and personal confrontation, then it's time to bring in others.
This could sound like "ganging up" on someone. That's certainly
how I read it at first. But then I gained this important insight. In
between steps one and two, a person has to explain what's going
on to other presumably trusted and wise spiritual siblings. These
other siblings in Christ aren't just "back up"—they're a reality
check on our own judgment. By this point, we should already be
asking ourselves if maybe we aren't seeing everything clearly and
need another perspective. If we've assessed the situation clearly
and confronted our spiritual sibling directly and lovingly, and yet
they aren't moved—then the addition of one or two others is as
much for us as it is for them. We'll need to choose siblings in
Christ who will tell us the truth, not just tell us what we want
to hear. This isn't the time to have our egos coddled, this is the
time to have our motives interrogated and our posture analyzed.
If, after that, others agree that we've appropriately fulfilled step
one—then they can accompany us into step two.

PROTO-CHURCH

If step two fails, then Jesus calls upon us to submit it to the assembly. This part is fascinating to me. We know that this Gospel we
call "Matthew" was written after Paul's letters. Yet it carries with it

traditions which predate Paul's church-planting journeys. So, here we have the author or authors of Matthew talking about a kind of proto-church. When Jesus first began to gather disciples, they themselves formed a community that wasn't yet the church we think of today, but was also distinct from the local Jewish synagogue. Wright calls this group, "little groups or cells of [Jesus's] followers meeting together, praying the prayers Jesus gave them, reminding one another of his teaching and trying to live it out . . . acting as small-scale, localized assemblies of God's renewed people".[2] *I love this!* This is what I picture when I think about the church. Jesus isn't talking about hauling someone before a tribunal of some bureaucratic institution. No! Jesus is talking about a small community of Jesus-disciples who are trying to live out the Jesus Way. That is who we submit ourselves to for accountability—not some corporate conglomerate that calls itself the Church with a capital "c."

I consider myself someone with a healthy distrust of authority. I've known more than my fair share of authority figures and entities who've used their power for selfish gain and ended up hurting others. So, when I read the verse about people being brought before the church, my hackles quickly get raised. But, honest to God, when we move beyond the corporate, bureaucratic, and institutional model of church and embrace this vision of God's kin(g)dom as a forged family of Jesus-disciples living out the Jesus Way, not only will I submit to their correction—*I want to!* I find myself wanting to be seen, known, and accountable to their loving vision. I want to be guided on the right path by this family. This is why, ever since I became a follower of Jesus, I've sought out mentors and communities that look like this—and I've found them. They're out there! They exist!

GENTILES AND TAX COLLECTORS

Finally, we have to tackle the hardest part of this passage: the final step. If a spiritual sibling won't even hear and receive the loving correction of their entire community of fellow siblings in Christ, then Jesus says we are to treat that person as we would a pagan or tax collector. This is a hard saying, mostly because it is easily misunderstood. It can easily sound like Jesus is reenacting the kind of insider/outsider barrier that his way of love has torn down. It could easily sound like Jesus is being punitive or exclusionary. But that's why our interpretation is so crucial. We need an ethical lens. That way we don't ascribe to Jesus something that is antithetical to his entire way of life. I love Mennonite pastor Melissa Florer-Bixler's comments on this verse in her book, *How to Have an Enemy*. She writes:

> Tax collectors and Gentiles are mentioned in this story of shaping church accountability because they operate within a different logic than that of Jesus. They operate outside a way of life shaped by God's covenantal love. Their commitments, the way they order their world, isn't compatible with the new order that Jesus initiates.[3]

There is so much wisdom in what Pastor Melissa is saying here. Jesus's reference to Gentiles and tax collectors isn't pejorative, as is often assumed. Gentiles and tax collectors were part of

Jesus's world, and he demonstrates love to them by sharing meals with them, healing them, and even praising their faith. Instead, this reference points to a distinction between two types of orders and logics. One way of organizing social life is through the exploitation of relationships, power hierarchies, and vengeance. That order is diametrically opposed to the way of Jesus. Jesus has shown us a new way of ordering our lives around the kind of love he's demonstrated. The Jesus Way disrupts hierarchies, overturns exploitation, and replaces vengeance with reconciliation. Jesus's way of love entails holistic accountability in community with other Jesus-disciples. Someone who rejects that way has opted out. Jesus isn't creating a wall of separation; Jesus is naming the reality that's being demonstrated. This person has chosen to operate outside the way of Jesus and the community of disciples, so that is how we must treat them—not as punishment, but as consent. We continue to treat them as Jesus has: with redeeming love and hope of return. But continuing to subject ourselves to harm caused by their words and actions violates the wisdom of setting up healthy boundaries.

That's why this framework Jesus gives us doesn't extend to abuse or oppression. Jesus isn't calling upon people who are in abusive relationships to follow this protocol. In cases like that, physical safety is the first priority. Once the person who has experienced abuse has their physical safety secured, and healthy boundaries are put in place, talk of forgiveness may follow. But full reconciliation may never be healthy or wise, depending on a whole host of complex factors. Jesus's reference to Gentiles and tax collectors gestures toward the boundaries of healthy community and the kind of commitment it requires.

6 | SWIMMING LESSONS

The Word became flesh and made his dwelling among us.
We have seen his glory, the glory of the one and only Son,
who came from the Father, full of grace and truth.

John 1:14–15[NIV]

MOVING TO "SIN CITY"

"You're moving where!?" Mama Scott asked incredulously. It was in between services on a Sunday morning, and I was still a pastoral intern, running around putting out little fires while trying to be friendly and welcoming. Mama Scott was a precious auntie from my home church, who even asked me to mentor her son at one point because he was beginning to act out in ways that concerned her. I knew she was from Louisiana, but we hadn't discussed it much beyond that. She'd either overheard a conversation I'd had with someone else, or word was getting around the church.

"I'm moving to New Orleans!" I answered with excitement.

"That's Sin City!" she said.

With my body half-positioned as if to say, 'I'm on my way somewhere in a hurry,' I quipped, "I think you're thinking of Las Vegas."

"Well, I grew up in Laplace and we would never go into the city. Too much evil there." By this point, she'd leaned in a little and had a serious look on her face. I gave her words a couple seconds of thought.

"Oh, well, I'm moving there to attend a Bible college that specializes in urban ministry. And I've been down there twice with missions teams to evangelize during Mardi Gras."

"So you're going as a missionary?" This time she sounded more puzzled than concerned.

"Not really. I'm going to school to be trained in urban ministry, but I don't want to be a missionary. I want to live there, get to know people, and serve."

"Well, good luck!" she said. But I didn't really think she meant it.

At nineteen, I felt like I'd already lived a lifetime. I wasn't moving to New Orleans on a whim. I'd felt a calling to serve in the city, and while I was down there I felt a strong connection to the place, to the people, to the culture. But nothing could have prepared me for being fully immersed. New Orleans is a truly unique city, combining so many different cultural influences. Like the tributaries that flow into the Mississippi Delta on their way to the Gulf of Mexico, diverse cultures have flowed into New Orleans for generations. When I moved there in 2000, I was mostly ignorant of the city's extraordinary history. I didn't even know what a "second line" was, and I wasn't all that into seafood. What little I did know about New Orleans was mostly through hip-hop labels like No Limit and Cash Money Records. Add to that the many negative stereotypes I'd heard from the mission teams I'd evangelized with during Mardi Gras the two prior years. Before I'd even had a chance to settle in, there was already a lot for me to unlearn.

Over the next few years, as I lived, worked, and went to school in New Orleans, I developed a deep love for the city. I loved crawfish boils in City Park and Plum Street sno-balls (the best!). I loved hearing jazz bands play in the open air, and I even learned to love chicory coffee. But I also learned that there are two distinct sides to New Orleans: the tourist-facing side, and the rest. When someone visits New Orleans, much of what they're likely to see is a facade, like Main Street U.S.A. at Disney World. Of course I'm talking about the French Quarter, but also the hospitality industry in general. New Orleans survives on tourism that shrouds the city's acute inequity. The side of New Orleans I got to see was much less polished and performative. Instead, I served in a youth detention center, a men's homeless shelter, and many of the city's public housing developments, which by this time had earned nation-wide infamy as the neighborhoods where famous rappers were from. I learned that the official name of the "Magnolia Projects" was the C. J. Pete Public Housing Development while I was part of a team hosting weekly sidewalk Sunday school gatherings for children there. And while distributing bags of groceries and offering prayer in other neighborhoods, I learned that tens of thousands of New Orleans residents lived in housing so neglected by the city that it was barely suitable for human commencement address he once delivered called, "This Is Water." He begins by telling a version of a parable about two young fish who swim past an older, presumably wiser fish, and the older fish says, "Morning, boys. How's the water?" The two young fish swim on for a while, until one of them eventually asks, "What is 'water'?" Since it was a college commencement speech, a good deal of it has to do with the purpose of education. But in describing education as he sees it, Wallace begins to touch on a much deeper philosophy of freedom and perception. He describes freedom as the capacity to choose how to think about the meaning of one's own life and our view of others, and to act in unselfish ways. He even shares poignant insights on the value of worship and the destructive nature of idolatry (e.g., wealth, knowledge, sex, and power). What I keep coming back to is that waking up to our capacity to choose requires recognizing the water in which we're swimming: "The capital-T Truth is about life *before* death. It is about the real value of a real education, which has almost nothing to do with knowledge, and everything to do with simple awareness; awareness of what is so real and essential, so hidden in plain sight all around us, all the time, that we have to keep reminding ourselves over and over: 'This is water.' 'This is water.'"[1]

The philosophy of freedom Wallace outlines in this speech points to the everyday patterns of our lives that become normative and the ways our vision can be obscured by those norms. This is one of the most important keys to forging family: understanding culture. When we're oblivious to our cultural formation, we tend to assume its normative and correct, even divinely sanctioned. And that egocentrism is the source of so much relational conflict. But the truth is that all our cultures are a mixed bag. Some aspects of our cultures are wonderful, and some are insidiously evil. Culture isn't just one thing; culture is as complex and multifaceted as the people who create it.

Loving each other well entails learning about how and why we're culturally different and how to bridge our differences. We'll need to learn how to be a part of each others' lives in meaningful and life-giving ways. This means honoring each other's identities and discerning together how to navigate the waters of culture in which we all swim. We need swimming lessons. Following Jesus into a new kind of family requires paying attention to our culture and the cultures of others. It requires recognizing and resisting cultural assimilation while developing cultural dexterity. In the end, the culture of the new family we forge will be a beautiful hybrid that honors all people as the image of God.

SEEING THE RACIALIZED WATER WE SWIM IN

The first swimming lesson is understanding the difference between concepts that are often confused or confusing: concepts like race, ethnicity, and culture.

The United States is what sociologists Michael Emerson and Christian Smith called a "racialized" society in *Divided by Faith*. For centuries in the European colonies, then later in the newly formed United States of America, people were lumped together into racial categories such as "Black" and "White," based on highly subjective phenotypical features. These physical features are so infamously subjective that there arose the concept of "passing for White," in which a person could move from being labeled "Black" to being considered "White" by having fairer skin and straightened hair. This racial system of categorization was never innocent. From its beginning it was always a way of establishing a hierarchy that reinforced practices and political institutions like slavery and segregation. Pseudoscience was used to give the racial hierarchy an air of legitimacy. Nevertheless, biology has never supported the idea that different human races exist. As someone once said, "Race is like polyester; it's fake, but it's real."[2] The idea of different human races is an artificial construct. It's fake. But race has been so deeply encoded into American society (and beyond) through laws, customs, media, religion, and many other ways, that this artificial construct nevertheless exerts very real control over our lives.

Instead of different races, what we do find in human beings are diverse *ethnicities*. These are the particular ways in which human beings have adapted to their indigenous homes—the land and the plants and animals with which we share the land. Ethnicities produce variation in phenotypes, customs, language, and cultures. These are the natural ways humans fulfill God's command to tend and care for the creation of which we're called to be stewards. Culture is the cultivation of the earth. It's the application of our God-given intelligence, creativity, strength, and agency to the raw materials of human life with which God has entrusted us. Culture is like gardening, channelling the raw,

God-given capacity of life to grow, spread, blossom, flower, and bear fruit, so that life can flourish.

We can see this in scripture going all the way back to the first page. By placing humanity in a garden, the Genesis narrative is telling us that our calling as human beings is to care for and enhance the fruitfulness and flourishing of creation. In his highly practical book, *Many Colors*, Dr. Rah writes that Genesis 1:28 "reveals a connection between being made in the image of God and the ability to mirror God through the re-creation of God's image through culture. Genesis 1:28 reminds us that part of creation order is to go forth and create life, families, social systems, and cultures."[3] This blessing from God is God's calling of humans to partner with God in stewarding, ruling, and cultivating God's good world. Or, as Nancy Pearcey puts it,

> The first phrase, "be fruitful and multiply," means to develop the social world: build families, churches, schools, cities, governments, laws. The second phrase, "subdue the earth," means to harness the natural world: plant crops, build bridges, design computers, compose music. This passage is sometimes called the Cultural Mandate because it tells us that our original purpose was to create cultures, build civilizations.[4]

Culture is a developmental process of tending, caring, and cultivating creation. It's what we do with what we've been given by God. *Ethnicity* is what we call the collection of ways a group of people has learned to cultivate their portion of creation. It's the particular customs, language, and physical adaptations a people group has formed through their relationship to their historical and geographical context.

Due to the particular history of colonialism, slavery, and segregation in America, it's vitally important for Americans of European ancestry to understand how race has distorted the image of God. Instead of seeing the many beautiful and diverse ways human beings have cultivated their portion of creation and adapted by forming ethnicities, race was devised to categorize people based not on their ethnicity but on a few subjective physical features like skin color or hair texture. More than that, race combines people from vast swaths of diverse ethnicities into a larger category like "Black," and judges them as inferior to people from other vast swaths of diverse ethnicities, lumped together and called "White." This not only erases important ethnic distinctions between people groups, but it also unjustly advantages one racial group over all others: those deemed "White." This is the way race is related to the abhorrent idea of "White supremacy." White supremacy is the idea that people from diverse European ethnicities could discard their particularities and be combined into an amalgamated White race that is considered superior to all other races. Then this mythological superiority gets assumed and encoded into practices and policies that reinforce unjust social advantages.

Not only does this marginalize people who are not deemed White, it also erases meaningful distinctions among European ethnic groups. For example, when I was very young, I must have overheard someone at a family reunion mention that my mother's side of the family is Irish. This intrigued me because I knew next to nothing about Ireland or being Irish. So I asked my grandfather, "What does it mean that we're Irish? What do we do that's Irish?" My grandfather thought about it for a few seconds and then said, "Well, we celebrate St. Patrick's Day!"

I just stared at him in disbelief. "That's it?! Everybody does that!"

In response, he said, "Oh, then I guess we're just White."

Without realizing it, my grandfather had expressed something profoundly sad. At some point in the past, Irish immigrants in the United States had traded in their ethnic and cultural distinctiveness for the promise of greater social privilege as racially White. In so doing, we'd sacrificed all connection to our heritage. Perhaps if more Americans of European descent could learn how much of the distinct beauty of their diverse ethnicities has been lost to the intoxicating and destructive power of Whiteness, we would be better able to see the devastating effects of race and racism.

In addition to erasing ethnic distinctions, racialization has subjected people of African descent, Indigenous Americans, and people of other ethnic groups to dehumanization, violence, and oppression. Racialization created the idea that people labeled "Black," "Brown," "Red," or "Yellow" were less human than people deemed "White." This hierarchy of humanness was used as the justification for the enslavement of Africans, the forced removal and genocide of Native Americans, and a whole host of other racist atrocities. The racialization of American society and the myth of White supremacy destroys the image of God, opposes God's *shalom*, and is incompatible with following the Jesus Way.

MOVING BEYOND COLORBLIND CULTURE

For these reasons, some followers of Jesus have shifted to a "color-blind" approach. It can seem like the solution to race-based discrimination is to ignore race entirely, to pretend that racialization doesn't continue to exert powerful influence over society. White American Christians sometimes quote one particular line from Dr. Martin Luther King, Jr.'s "I Have a Dream" speech, while ignoring not just the rest of the speech, but the entirety of his life's work. When Dr. King said, "I have a dream that my four little children will one day live in a nation where they will not be judged by the color of their skin but by the content of their character,"[5] he didn't mean that this dream can be realized by simply pretending not to notice people's physical characteristics and the way they've been racially categorized. He certainly didn't mean that "not seeing color" would redress the dehumanizing ways African Americans have been treated, the system of segregation, or their lack of access to the vote. His point was precisely the opposite. Unless and until the injustices perpetuated by America's racial hierarchy are dismantled, there can never be a future in which his children would not be discriminated against based upon their racial designation.

The glaring problem with the colorblind approach is that it's a lie. We do "see" race because we've been taught to. But when society is structured in a way that caters to the racialized group with the most political power, it becomes so normalized that it's invisible, like water to a fish. To aim for a colorblind culture, then, is to default to the cultural assumptions of those deemed White.

This is precisely what happened to Dr. Richard Twiss, a Lakota-Sioux pastor and theologian who went to be with the Creator in 2013. In his book *One Church, Many Tribes: Following Jesus the Way God Made You,* he draws attention to one of the ways the colorblind approach harms people. Like many Native American Christians in the United States, Dr. Twiss was initially taught to reject his ethnic and cultural heritage. He was taught that to be a follower of Jesus he had to give up all Lakota-Sioux practices, his Native language, and even cut his long hair. He tells the tragic story of when he was a new Christian, and he asked a White pastor how he should navigate the relationship between his Native identity and Christian identity. He writes,

> I distinctly remember him opening the Bible he was carrying and reading from Galatians 3:28 (NIV), where Paul wrote, "There is neither Jew nor Greek, slave nor free, male nor female, for you are all one in Christ Jesus." After reading the passage, this pastoral leader commented on how cultures should all blend together for us as Christians. He then concluded, "So, Richard, don't worry about being Indian; just be like us."[6]

That response: "Just be like us," is an excellent example of what can happen when someone doesn't see the cultural waters they're swimming in. This White pastor advising Dr. Twiss didn't realize that "being like him" necessarily involves participating in and adopting certain cultural practices, practices particular to his White culture. He didn't realize that forfeiting his own ethnic and cultural heritage would rob Dr. Twiss of a beautiful and precious gift given to him by God.

To forge family in the way of Jesus requires moving beyond colorblind culture. Forged families recognize and appreciate the many beautiful ways God's image has been reflected through our ethnicities and cultural practices. Forged families also recognize the ways racialization has unjustly advantaged those ethnicities amalgamated into Whiteness over those left out. To forge family it's necessary to confront racial injustice in society and counteract it. Forged families are those that can see the cultural waters in which we're all swimming and learn how to swim together.

HIP-HOP AND CULTURAL HYBRIDITY

The greatest gift I've been given to help me traverse complex cultural waters is growing up immersed in hip-hop culture. From its birth 50 years ago in the Bronx, hip-hop has been a highly inclusive and adaptive cultural movement. Not only is hip-hop boldly and proudly about calling attention to the struggle of African Americans in over-policed and under-resourced neighborhoods, it is also a celebration of the ways people of diverse ethnicities and cultures come together to express themselves artistically and joyfully.

Few people embody that more than Efrain "Brother E" Alicea. A self-described "Nuyorican" (New York–Puerto Rican) and founder of Elements Church, Brother E was a hip-hop pioneer who passed away in 2023. For over a decade, he and I grew in our friendship to the point that we considered each other spiritual family. When my family was living in Boston and his in New York, our families would meet up and spend time together each year at a family camp in New Hampshire called Pilgrim Pines. We'd also make time for each other once a year at a conference for pastors in Chicago called Midwinter.

Brother E was a hip-hop aficionado. He was an emcee himself but was also one of the founders of the longest running Christian hip-hop festival in New York history, called Rap Fest. He was there at the beginning, a teenager in the Bronx, when the hip-hop movement burst onto his block. That's why, in 2016, when Netflix released a television show about the birth of hip-hop in the Bronx called "The Get Down," I called him to do an interview about what it was like to be there back then, and how it compared to the portrayal on the show. He had a lot to say about the show and hip-hop, as he always did. But what stuck out to me most in that interview was how hopeful hip-hop made him feel as kid because it embraced him as he was, someone who felt like a misfit—too Puerto Rican for his block but too American when he went to visit relatives in Puerto Rico. He describes the first time he remembers feeling a part of hip-hop culture as the moment he first heard "Rappers Delight" by the Sugar Hill Gang on the radio. When Wonder Mike says, "To the Black, to the White, the Red, and the Brown, the Purple and Yellow," Brother E says that in that moment he connected with the movement because of its inclusivity. His friend group was diverse, and so were those who were building this new cultural movement: breakdancers, graffiti artists, deejays, and emcees. For Brother E, hip-hop was a revelation because it celebrated the beautiful cultural variations of all the people it included, while building something brand new. I knew exactly what he meant because that's what it was for me too.

Growing up, hip-hop culture provided a common space for me to learn from and share with people of different ethnicities and cultures. But hip-hop is decidedly not colorblind; it directly confronts the destructive power of racialization in American society and beyond, condemning the injustices caused by racism. Hip-hop incorporates the creative cultural expressions of people from a wide range of ethnicities and simultaneously forms a new cultural movement. This is an example of what Brian Bantum has called "cultural hybridity."[7] He points out that it's common to think of culture as static and that through multiculturalism, cultures can exist side by side while preserving their distinctiveness. But Brian is biracial himself, both Black and White, and married to Gail Song Bantum, who is Korean American. In his theological work he's explored how his own life and family demonstrates that cultures aren't static, but dynamic. The culture he brings to his family as a biracial person is honored along with his partner Gail's Korean American culture. They appreciate and adopt aspects of each other's cultures, and together they create a new hybrid culture within their family that they then share with others.[8] This is actually how culture has always worked.

Cultures evolve, adapt, and change. Cultures aren't fixed, but dynamically incorporate aspects of other cultures, creating cultural hybridity. When we understand this about how culture works, it's like learning how to do the backstroke. We're dis-abused of the notion that our culture was ever monolithic in the first place, but rather has always been a compilation of influences adapted over time. Then we can open ourselves up to learning and sharing our culture with others, while counteracting the unjust distribution of power that stems from the history of racial-ization. Through this equitable cultural exchange, we're forging a new way of being spiritual family.

JESUS AND INCARNATIONAL CULTURE

If it hadn't been for Jesus and hip-hop, I never would have moved to New Orleans at nineteen. And then I wouldn't have learned what "incarnation" is really all about. Jesus reveals a God who isn't scandalized by the particularities of our ethnici-ties or cultures. Jesus was full human and as such had ethnicity and culture. Jesus was a Judean born in first-century Judea-Palestine. He wasn't part of some amalgamated White race. Rather, he was part of the Jewish people who at that time were ruled over by the Roman empire. As the Civil Rights luminary Howard Thurman wrote in *Jesus and the Disinherited*, "the fact is that Jesus of Nazareth was a Jew of Palestine [. . .] The second important fact for our consideration is that Jesus was a poor Jew. [. . .] The third fact that Jesus was a member of a minor-ity group in the midst of a larger dominant and controlling group."[9] Jesus's ethnicity and culture aren't incidental; they are exactly what God wanted them to be. Through Jesus, we see God identifying with our full humanity, even more so the masses of disinherited human beings who struggle to survive under oppression.

Jesus shows us the love of God that enters into our culture, shares it with us, and creates something new. Jesus births a movement of love so inclusive that today his disciples are members of every nation on earth. They are not called upon to leave behind what makes them distinct members of their particular ethnic groups: their customs, their cultural practices, their language, their homeland. They are called upon to bring all of who they are into God's kin(g)dom so that God can gather them all up and glorify them.

> *The [New Jerusalem] does not need the sun or the moon to shine on it, for the glory of God gives it light, and the Lamb is its lamp. The nations will walk by its light, and the kings of the earth will bring their splendor into it. On no day will its gates ever be shut, for there will be no night there. The glory and honor of the nations will be brought into it.* (Revelation 21:23–26[NIV])

The beautifully diverse ways that human beings have cultivated the earth, developed culture, and express their ethnicity glorifies God. That is why those cultural expressions are pictured in the New Creation:

> *After this I looked, and there before me was a great multitude that no one could count, from every nation, tribe, people and language, standing before the throne and before the Lamb. They were wearing white robes and were holding palm branches in their hands.* (Revelation 7:9[NIV])

The kin(g)dom of God is a city not unlike New Orleans. It's a unique society precisely because of the many cultural influences that have combined to make it what it is. The particularities of every people group are tributaries that flow into the very presence of the Lamb and are celebrated for their glorious splendor. Forging family in the way of Jesus means learning how to swim in those kin(g)dom waters.

7 | IN THIS FAMILY, WE...

This, then, is how you should pray:
'Our Father in heaven,
hallowed be your name,
your kingdom come,
your will be done,
on earth as it is in heaven.
Give us today our daily bread.
And forgive us our debts,
as we also have forgiven our debtors.
And lead us not into temptation,
but deliver us from the evil one.'

Matthew 6:9–13[NIV]

UPROOTED BY KATRINA

"T. C., you staying or leaving?" they asked, but I had no answer. I was already starting to feel nervous. It was my second year serving on the small staff of a faith-based community center called Trinity Christian Community (TCC), located in an under-resourced neighborhood of New Orleans called Hollygrove. It was a

Saturday, and we were scheduled to have a yard sale outside the center, so I joined the rest of the team early that morning to help with preparations. But there was a huge elephant in the room that none of us could ignore: a hurricane in the Gulf of Mexico named Katrina.

Even though everyone on the team loved New Orleans, and especially loved Hollygrove, not all of us had the same feelings about sticking around during hurricanes. Half of the team were from out of state like me. We didn't have family roots in the city, and we didn't own any property. We were there because of a sense of calling, even if that calling was temporary. If a hurricane was headed toward New Orleans, we had no problem getting out of its way. At the same time, we felt strong sense of loyalty to the neighborhood and especially the team.

It was that shared sense of calling that made serving at TCC such a life-transforming experience. Our deep friendships were forged by serving alongside one another and depending on each other, and through in-depth discussions about what it means to love one another. Together we read and discussed a book on racial reconciliation entitled *Grace Matters*, written by Spencer Perkins and Chris Rice. Five members of the team were White and five were Black, and some of the discussions got tense. Together we unpacked what we really mean by "systemic racism." These were not things that were taught at the Bible college I graduated from.

We were also forged into family by the ministry's leadership. Kevin Brown, the executive director, Earl Williams, and Evelyn Turner were amazing role models. They invested in us personally, individually, but also as a team. The way they encouraged and relied on each other showed us how to be a better team. They taught us the true meaning of community, even when all the pretensions of church are stripped away. That morning, we were working together to pull off this yard sale with the kind of unconscious teamwork that comes from earned trust.

As we gathered items for sale and set up tables to display them on, radio reports kept interrupting the music to describe the path of the storm. There was a lot of speculation, not just among the staff, but also on the radio. It seemed like new models of where the storm would make landfall were being reported every few minutes. Some of the reports weren't sure if it would be a direct hit or complete miss. But almost exactly one year before, hurricane Ivan had been bearing down on New Orleans, and the reports then were sure it was going to be "the big one." "They always say that!" someone was sure to say. Ivan eventually missed New Orleans by a small margin.

Everyone who's ever lived in New Orleans knows what would happen if "the big one" ever actually hit directly. People would casually say, "New Orleans would fill up like a *punch bowl,*" because of how deep below sea level the city sits. So, naturally, the year before, when Ivan was threatening to strike the city, Osheta and I evacuated with our toddler-aged son. We ended up feeling duped when the storm barely caused any damage. Our friends who were born and raised in New Orleans teased us. To hear them tell it, they hadn't been scared at all. Our elderly next-door neighbor recited to us a long list of all the hurricanes she'd survived. The one that sticks out in my mind was hurricane Betsy, which I'm told did significant damage.

As the radio warned residents to begin making evacuation plans, I could sense tension building among the staff. Half the staff paid little mind to the warnings. Hurricane season is as typical of New Orleans culture as Mardi Gras. So, they carried on, business as usual. But for the out-of-town staff members, this was much scarier. I started imagining what it would be like to be stuck in our second-floor apartment with flood waters rising downstairs, trapping us. I started imagining what it would be like trying to get to safety with our three-year-old son and Osheta, now eight months pregnant.

"Nope. Not going through that!" I thought.

But I still wasn't entirely sold on the threat of Katrina. What if this was just another false alarm? Between the paltry stipend I was paid to serve at TCC and the few small church websites I'd managed to design in recent weeks, my income was small. We really couldn't afford to take another spur-of-the-moment mini-vacation. Nevertheless, the cons of staying far outweighed the pros. So I left work early to go home and talk with Osheta. If we were going to leave, we were going to need to pack up quickly and prepare to get on the road as soon as possible.

That night, as we made our plans, we thought about our friends, Jason and Jennifer. They'd recently begun attending the same Presbyterian church as us and lived close by in Mid-city. Jason had been a volunteer at TCC for several years and had been a part of my book study group at church. We knew they didn't own a vehicle and that we had just enough room for them in our minivan. So we called and asked them to evacuate with us. At first they politely declined, but we insisted, and eventually they relented. We agreed that we'd see them in the morning.

We only packed the essentials we thought we'd need for a two-to-three-day stay in southeast Texas, where Osheta is from. We took a few changes of clothes, important documents like birth certificates, and the tower of my kit-built PC that I used to design websites. Only days before, I'd installed a message board on the church's website, and I had several other clients who I thought might try to contact me.

We said to ourselves, "We'll be smart. We'll get up at 5 a.m. and beat the traffic." Unfortunately, so did half of New Orleans! Mayor Ray Nagin ordered the first mandatory evacuation in New Orleans's history, and traffic on Interstate 10 heading east was redirected west in an initiative called "Contraflow." That meant that as we ascended the onramp at 5 a.m. that Sunday morning, August 28, 2005, we drove directly into a line of cars as far as the eye could see. The drive to southeast Texas that normally took no more than seven hours, now with hundreds of thousands of New Orleans residents evacuating the city all at once, turned into bumper-to-bumper traffic for *20 hours!*

The scene of our family evacuating New Orleans sounds like the set-up for a joke. Crammed in our small Plymouth Voyager minivan were Osheta (eight months pregnant), myself, our three-year-old son, our two friends, our pet cat named Tiger, and their pet "fancy rat" named *Gatto* (cat in Spanish). You can't make this stuff up! And maybe it would have been funnier at the time if we weren't so scared and uncertain of what to do next.

When we finally reached southeast Texas, Osheta's god-parents, Mickey and Missy Lane, opened their home to our entire motley crew. It was an incredibly loving demonstration of hospitality. And for the next several days, along with many millions of other Americans, we were glued to the television, watching the news intently as Katrina made landfall and reporters tried to assess the damage. I don't think anyone was prepared to witness what happened when the levees broke. It was entirely surreal.

Day after day, I was filled with anger and heartache as every major news outlet showed photos and video footage of my New Orleanian neighbors being left for dead by their own government. Tens of thousands of people were herded into the Superdome and the Convention Center and provided with minimal care. People were trapped inside attics, being air-lifted off rooftops, and rescued from toxic floodwaters.

Somewhere in all the news coverage, I happened to see a photo of an Italian restaurant I recognized from the same street in Mid-city Jason and Jennifer lived on. The floodwater was up to the sign above the door. I found out later that the floodwaters in Hollygrove were just as high, if not higher.

Long after everyone else in the house had enough of the bad news, I couldn't pull myself away from the screen. Questions kept swirling in my mind. *How are we going to get back? Would there be anything left?*

That's when I heard the words that changed everything. "City officials say it could be weeks, possibly months, before residents will be allowed back into the city."

"What did they just say?" I asked incredulously. No one else was paying attention.

"Did you hear what they just said? It sounded like they said 'weeks, possibly months' before we can go home. But that can't be right, right?"

Now, everyone was watching. Eventually, they reiterated. The city has been closed to residents while relief agencies, federal, and state agencies send workers to the city. FEMA, a week too late, had finally shown up, and "Brownie" (the nickname President George W. Bush gave to FEMA chief Michael Brown) was *not* doing a "heck of a job."

That's when it hit me: We were effectively homeless. Our apartment, with nearly all of our most cherished possessions, was gone. And we didn't have "weeks, possibly months" to wait. We had a baby on the way imminently! Paralyzing fear rushed in on the heels of a thousand questions. *Where are we going to have this baby? Where are we going to live? How would we afford to live there? How would we even get there?* It felt like there were more questions than air to breathe.

The next few days were filled with a lot of prayer and tears. We talked with friends and mentors from all over the country. And a lot of people called to make sure we were okay. But we weren't; we were in crisis. In our darkest moments of despair we would lament to one another, "Where is God in all this?" Or "how can God allow this to happen?" At some point, we just hit a wall and broke down. The fear, the uncertainty, the sadness was too heavy for us to bear. We collapsed on the floor next to the bed trying to pray through sobs. We didn't know how to pray anymore, so we just cried out.

That's when our pastor, Mike Hogg, called. He wanted to let us know he was organizing a gathering in Houston of members who'd evacuated to the west of Louisiana. Not everyone was able to use their cell phones with New Orleans area codes, probably due to damaged cell towers. The online message board I'd installed a few weeks earlier was now the primary way displaced church members were keeping in touch with one another.

As we gathered in the parking lot of a strip mall, prayed with one another, cried on each others' shoulders, and swapped stories, I saw the body of Christ form before my very eyes. Pastor Mike shepherded a flock of scared sheep, scattered by a storm, and unsure of what to do next. Words fail when I think of just how lost we would have been had it not been for the body of Christ surrounding us. In the midst of those dark days, the only glimmers of hope came from prayer and conversations with friends who'd become family. We felt the miraculous love of God in the voices and embraces of our siblings in Christ.

In fact, our next steps after the storm came from two siblings in Christ who'd been classmates of mine in Bible college: Jimi and Melissa Orekoya. They'd moved to Boston after graduation to attend seminary. Jimi and I had both talked about going to seminary after Bible college, but I'd put it off to serve in Hollygrove. Jimi called and said, "Come to Massachusetts. This state will take care of you!" He and Mel said we could stay with them until we got on our feet. Hope began to break through like beams of light streaming in through a window. Maybe Boston could be a new start.

We left Texas with a mixture of fear and faith in our stomachs. To bolster our resolve, we planned a support-raising road trip with stops along the way where we could visit friends and members of our forged family. They prayed with us and gave us generous financial gifts, baby clothes, and encouragement. We experienced such an amazing outpouring of love and support from the family of God that by the time we reached Massachusetts, we were already beginning to believe Boston could be our new home.

When we arrived in Massachusetts, we were told we needed to register at an Air Force base down in Cape Cod in order to receive benefits from FEMA and assistance from Red Cross. When we arrived, I saw a fragile-looking folding table with a plain piece of paper taped to it that simply said "Housing." I kept one foot pointing away as I very reluctantly approached. "What kind of 'housing' are you offering?" I asked.

"Where do you want to live?" the man behind the table asked in response, in a thick New Englander accent.

This was my first time east of Ohio, so everything I knew about Boston came from movies and TV. The only thing I could think of was, "Harvard is in Cambridge." So I blurted out, "I hear Cambridge is nice!"

He leafed through a stack of papers on his clipboard. "Would you like a two-bedroom, or a three-bedroom?"

"Umm . . . three-bedroom," I said like it was a question.

"Okay, just sign here and we'll contact you in a few days."

Two weeks later we were moving into a three-bedroom townhouse in Cambridge, a five-minute bus ride from Harvard Square.

Our evacuation from New Orleans because of hurricane Katrina changed our lives forever. God met us in our darkest and most fear-filled days through the body of Christ. God showed us more love and care than we'd ever experienced before. We'll always love New Orleans, and we thank God for the many wonderful friendships that were forged there. Most of all, we experienced forged family showing up for us. Even still, being uprooted from everything we'd come to know as home severely disoriented us. We'd have to learn how to be family again in a new home.

FORMATIVE RHYTHMS

Human beings are meaning-making creatures. And one of the most important ways we make meaning in our lives is by how we mark time. Boston is really where our family began to settle into formative rhythms. We dove headlong into the practices that mark the changing seasons. We went apple-picking every fall, spent time in a cabin by a lake in the summers, and went sledding in the winters. Just like a river carves a path through the valley shaping and reshaping its boundaries over the course of years, our seasonal rhythms in Boston formed us as a family.

Each summer Osheta would choose a theme to explore with the kids. Sometimes that theme just popped into her head, and she decided unilaterally what it would be. Other years, the kids lobbied her for their choice. The summer I remember most vividly was the "summer of myths." Our middle son, T. J., has always been fascinated by mythologies. So that summer was his dream come true. We read mythology books and went exploring Boston in search of myths. We visited islands a ferry ride across the harbor and pretended they were the isles of ancient Grecian voyages.

Another anchoring practice for us was reading before bed each night. We read through the entire *Chronicles of Narnia* series one chapter at a time, twice. We also spent at least one week in New Hampshire at camp each summer. We'd sit by the lake, swim, roast marshmallows, and get attacked by mosquitos.

Practices like these form the character of a family's identity. They're what shape our life together and point to our purpose.

OUR ABBA

Jesus has given his disciples a family-forging rhythm in the form of the "Our Father" prayer. This prayer has been prayed, studied, dissected, explained, re-explained, parts of it rejected, and so on, for going on two thousand years. And, to this day, we still haven't exhausted its depth, its genius, its power to shape, form, and move us. The "Our Father" is an amazing treasure that no one person, church, or tradition can lay hold of entirely. Instead, we stand before this gift in awe and hope to catch a glimpse of just what Jesus might have been getting at when he taught his disciples to pray this way.

The very first line requires us to consider Jesus's audacious claim on God. Granted, God had been referred to as Israel's Father in the Hebrew Bible. But scholars who've researched the rabbinical traditions of the Second Temple period of Judaism in which Jesus lived overwhelmingly agree that no rabbi before Jesus offered this view of God as Father to their disciples for them to embrace for themselves. And there was definitely no rabbi before Jesus who offered it to both male and female disciples. Unique to Jesus is placing God-as-Father center stage and inviting his disciples into this type of familial relationship with God and one another.

In fact, more than "Lord" or "God," "Father" is the primary way Jesus addresses God throughout his recorded ministry in the Gospels. In his famous Gethsemane prayer, when he sweated great drops of blood, Jesus prays to his *Abba*. Jesus took communicating, interacting, and relating with God out of the ceremonial context of the temple or the performance-based context of Pagan religion, and places it firmly in the intimate, tender context of family life. Jesus reveals a God who is like a father who loves us, smiles over us, and is proud of us. And by beginning this prayer *"our* Father," Jesus invites us into a communal practice, reimagining ourselves as part of God's family. Such practices are especially important in our lives when we're trying to set a new trajectory toward liberation and healing, out of dysfunction and dangerous behaviors.

REIMAGINING RAPHAEL

A few years ago I was serving young men who were court-involved through a diversion program based in North Minneapolis. I was part of a team that provided these teens support through case management, group dialogue, and circle practices. The hope was that through this diversion program, we could disrupt cycles that kept them stuck in the court system and at high risk for injury or even death because, soberingly, many of the young men I worked with were routinely involved in gun violence. Some of these youth were fully aware that if something didn't change, they could easily become part of another tragic story, like Raphael's.

Raphael was a young man ready to make a change and chart a new course for his life. He'd been gang-involved and caught up in gun violence, but he confessed to our team that he was ready to leave that life behind. He was nearly halfway through the three-month program when I took some time off from Christmas until just after the New Year. But the week before Christmas, Raphael had begun to really opening up during groups I facilitated on subjects like "Masculinity in the Media" and "Exploring Emotions." He told us about how his sister had been involved in an awful car accident that resulted in her being hospitalized in a coma. She'd been riding with some boys in a stolen car, and they were chased by police and then crashed. His sister's accident, combined with his own cases, had Raphael reevaluating his life. He shared with us how he'd been praying for his sister while she was in the hospital and how he'd been thinking about how "enough is enough," he wanted a new life. On his arm he had tattooed a quote he loved, "The future belongs to those who believe in the beauty of their dreams." He said that he was ready to believe and dream again. We were all really impressed as he vulnerably shared about how he was ready to take all the necessary steps to make that happen, like cutting off negative influences in his life.

This was a Thursday, when each week we would invite a graduate of the program named Lewiee to come back and share with the youth. Since he'd graduated from the program, Lewiee had achieved a lot of success. He'd become a well-known hip-hop artist in the Twin Cities, started his own collective of artists as a business, and began working with the county to help officials and legislators rethink our local juvenile justice system. Lewiee typically shared about his experiences and dropped pearls of practical wisdom. But Lewiee is also proudly "spiritual, not religious." He's adamant about his disconnection from organized religion. Lewiee was there that Thursday when Raphael was opening up like this, and we were both ready to capitalize on this opportunity. Lewiee went first. He started to tell Raphael, "Not only do you need to cut off those negative influences that are going to drag you back to your old life, you also need to surround yourself with people who, like you, are on a mission to do something positive with their lives. You need others around you who can motivate you and encourage you to keep going on the path you're now on."

Lewiee began to share about the group of friends he's connected with and how they encourage one another. Then he said, "You should get together with those friends on a regular basis— like every week! And not only should you get together with them, but you should also cultivate some practices of self-care, meditation, spiritual groundedness, and think about ways to uplift the community."

At this point, you can probably imagine my face. I couldn't contain my amusement. Even Lewiee quickly realized that what he'd been describing was starting to sound *very* religious. So he throws out an abrupt disclaimer: "I'm not talking about church!"

But it was too late, I was already laughing out loud. It turns out that two-thousand-year-old rhythms of community and spiritual practices have intuitive and enduring wisdom.

Unfortunately, Raphael was never given a chance to implement that wisdom. On New Year's Eve he was shot to death in an alley over a dispute about the sale of his Balenciaga shoes, worth over $1,000. When detectives arrived on the scene, Raphael's body was found shoeless. When we met with Raphael's mother, I had the honor of giving her a painting I made of him that featured the quote he'd shared with us that Thursday evening. She thanked me warmly through tears, squeezed me tight, and used the image on the t-shirts worn at his funeral.

RHYTHMS OF RESURRECTION

A new life's trajectory like the one Raphael was poised to embark upon requires sustaining rhythms and practices in community. This is what the early church in Acts illustrates. The power of the liberating Spirit that raised Jesus from the dead still animates the Jesus movement to this very day. But we often overlook the fact that when the Spirit gets ahold of people, they get forged into a new way of being human community together—a new kind of family that transcends the artificial social divisions erected by the world gone wrong. The liberating Spirit destroys those dividing walls and forges a Jesus family that is in the process of becoming more and more like Jesus—a Jesus family that is pulsing with the power of the resurrection. This pulsing power is then sustained though rhythms of life that nourish and equip.

The Jesus movement coalesces into Jesus communities that have Jesus-centered embodied practices.

Embodied practices are primal. Before you and I are verbal creatures, and even before we are creatures who have conscious thoughts, we're embodied creatures who occupy space and move through the world. Before we could talk or even had object permanence, we were held by our caregivers, fed by our caregivers, and carried by our caregivers. Before we could say "mama" or "dada," much less conceptualize what a parent is, someone was tending to our physical needs. Our embodied experiences are the bedrock of our thoughts and words, which become our habits and character, which shape our life's trajectory. Our embodied experiences are forming us, whether we realize it or not.

That is why becoming a family isn't merely a matter of calling each other "sister" and "brother," and it's not merely a matter of thinking of one another as family, as real and important as those things are. More fundamentally, we have to have shared experiences that bond us with one another. And those shared experiences can't simply be twice a year on Christmas and Easter. The people who become family for us are those with whom we've shared rhythms of life—practices that endure through seasons of life and stand the test of time.

Forging family takes practice. It doesn't happen overnight. We have to share formative practices over an extended period of time that leave a lasting impression on our souls. That doesn't mean it has to take our whole lives, but that also means it will take longer than one hour a week or twice a year. If we're to follow the way of Jesus into forged family, we will have to have a set of core practices that we routinely participate in. The Jesus family that was forged in first-century Judea-Palestine had these, as the book of Acts reports:

> *They devoted themselves to the apostles' teaching and to fellowship, to the breaking of bread and to prayer. Everyone was filled with awe at the many wonders and signs performed by the apostles. All the believers were together and had everything in common. They sold property and possessions to give to anyone who had need. Every day they continued to meet together in the temple courts. They broke bread in their homes and ate together with glad and sincere hearts, praising God and enjoying the favor of all the people. And the Lord added to their number daily those who were being saved.* (Acts 2:42–47NIV)

God's redemptive movement in scripture follows a pattern: God's blessing comes to rest upon a family who becomes a vehicle for God's blessing to be extended beyond themselves to the whole world. What we see in Acts chapter 2 is the birth of the new covenant version of this family blessing. A new way of being human community is forming. And this new formation wasn't merely a matter of new words or new thoughts—as important as those are—it required new embodied practices.

The Jesus family devoted themselves to the apostles' teaching, to the fellowship, the breaking of bread, and to the prayers, four categories of practices that began to form this new family. It didn't happen instantly, but over time. This new community began to share their lives with one another. They began to make memories together. They began to have unique shared experiences.

The early church gathered together on the first day of the week for worship because that was the day of the week when Jesus rose from the dead. And it was also the first day of the new creation. In Genesis, the poetic story about God creating the world says that God labored for six days and rested on the seventh day. The new covenant begins a new era of creation, a new Sunday, with Jesus as the first fruits of the new creation.

The passage also tells us that the early Jesus-disciples gathered in a public place (the temple courts) and also gathered in their homes. They had public worship and fellowship gatherings, and they had private worship and fellowship gatherings. They shared meals together as Jesus had modeled for them, and they had a favorable public witness that led to their growth. It also says they shared their possessions and met each others' needs.

In his magisterial commentary on Acts, Dr. Willie James Jennings homes in on the word "common" in this passage. This new way of generosity wasn't merely a giving of financial resources, it was a giving of oneself to form a new life together.

A new kind of giving is exposed at this moment, one that binds bodies together as the first reciprocal donation where the followers give themselves to one another. The possessions will follow. What was at stake here was not the giving up of all possessions but the giving up of each one, one by one as the Spirit gave direction, and as the ministry of Jesus made demand. Thus anything they had that might be used to bring people into sight and sound of the incarnate life, anything they had that might be used to draw people to life together and life itself and away from the reign of poverty, hunger, and despair—such things were subject to being given up to God. The giving is for the sole purpose of announcing the reign of the Father's love through the Son in the bonds of communion together with the Spirit.[1]

This new shared life in Christ forges a bond that breaks the powers of death through self-donating love. It's not magic—it doesn't happen in flash or with the wave of a wand. It takes practice. It takes rhythms of gathering, eating, giving, teaching, sending, serving. It takes seasons of plenty and seasons of want, giving and receiving, donating, collecting, blessing. This new family creates new traditions that are unique to them.

Many people today feel disconnected and adrift, like they're all alone and don't have anywhere they belong. They don't need another religious institution, they need a community that forges strangers into family. They need the revelation that there is a God in heaven who smiles over them, calls them beloved, and invites them into the family of God. It is the embodied practices and rhythms that will sustain the powerful new life from the Spirit. So it turns out those kitschy signs we might see in a craft supply store that say "In this family, we . . ." are on to something.

In this family, we . . . *Love one another as beloved siblings. Share all things in common, meeting one another's needs. Ground ourselves in embodied spiritual practices. Learn wisdom from our elders and empower the rising generation. Dream and work together toward God's future shalom.*

8 | GIVING SPECIAL HONOR

The King will reply,
"Truly I tell you, whatever you did
for one of the least of these brothers and sisters of mine,
you did for me."

Matthew 25:40[NIV]

THE PULSE MASSACRE

As the news began to spread of another mass shooting, this time in Orlando, Florida, like many other Americans I was heart-broken and furious. Forty-nine precious lives were taken that night in a gruesome attack that has forever changed that city and each of the families or friends who lost loved ones. The Pulse night-club massacre on June 12, 2016, also marked a turning point in my relationship to the LGBTQ+ community. It pierced my heart and challenged me to confront my own prejudices. It prompted me to ask what the love of Jesus looks like in my life and ministry toward members of the LGBTQ+ community.

That day we began planning a prayer vigil to be hosted in the church offices. Our church community had developed a practice of prayer and lament each time there was a tragedy blanketing the headlines and gripping our hearts. We'd publicly pray during our Sunday morning worship gathering, we'd hold a prayer meeting in the church offices where there was an informal gathering space, and we'd offer individuals and families an opportunity to meet with a pastor to pray. Hosting this kind of prayer vigil—one of deep lament over a tragic loss of life—had become an important part of my ministry. It was one of my first pastoral assignments after arriving in Los Angeles to serve among a multiethnic and socioeconomically diverse congregation that gathered downtown.

I was a newly installed associate pastor when we got the news that a trans woman had been murdered in Skid Row. Her named was Kourtney, she was a Black woman, and she was shot to death by an intimate partner. A team of us from the church gathered together with her friends and neighbors on a street corner in Skid Row to console one another and remember her. As memories of her were shared, I thought about how Kourtney lived in a social location of so many overlapping marginal identities. Identities are complex, of course, but we know Kourtney was a resident of Skid Row, living in supportive housing for chronically unhoused individuals, and that neighbors that evening said she'd once lived with them on the streets. This meant that she would have had to navigate those dangers while trying to save up and find a housing placement. Also, Kourtney was a Black, transgender woman. In any one of these aspects of her social location she was unjustly disadvantaged in society. Together, all three made her particularly vulnerable—a vulnerability grievously confirmed by her violent murder. I kept thinking about how so many people live with this kind of social vulnerability every day.

When our community gathered together in the church offices after the Pulse massacre for a prayer vigil, two beloved queer members of our community led us in prayers that brought waves of sadness and lament, but also bold declarations of resistance and a refusal to bow down to hopelessness. This was the first time I can remember being ministered to by my queer siblings in Christ, and it changed me. It challenged me to scrutinize the ways I'd been complicit in marginalizing members of the LGBTQ+ community through policies and theologies that relegated them to second-class status within the church and in society at large. It sent me back to the scriptures with a Jesus-shaped ethical lens that broadened my perspective on God's love. Since then, I've had more time and space to reflect on how forging family in the way of Jesus entails giving special honor to those members of the body who occupy marginalized social locations. I believe this is an essential part of how we put on display the powerfully countercultural love of Jesus—the kin(g)dom of God.

WIDOWS, SEX WORKERS, AND EUNUCHS

Throughout Jesus's ministry, he constantly drew attention to those on the margins of society. Those he highlighted could be marginalized for a whole host of reasons. Some were cast aside because they weren't considered worthy contributors to society.

Maybe they were persons who had been born with a condition that made it more difficult for them to walk. Or maybe they were deaf or hard of hearing. In a society where there were very few, if any, social safety nets, this would subject a person to severe vulnerability. The same goes for widows. In Jesus's context, many women were dependent upon men for subsistence, whether from a father, husband, or some other male provider. Older women who'd been dependent upon their husbands or sons their whole lives, but had been widowed, were threatened by extreme vulnerability. Not only did Jesus honor people from marginalized groups (e.g., "blessed are the poor," Luke 6:20), he also condemned the way society unjustly disadvantaged them.

For example, some have seen the mite-giving widow from Mark 12 and Luke 21 as a lesson on generosity, but that doesn't seem to be Jesus's overall point. Jesus's commendation of the widow was a stinging rebuke of the rich who'd given before her. While their gifts were donated from their surplus, hers was sacrificial. But even more foundational to his point was her poverty. Why did she have so little in the first place? The previous verse in Luke's telling says, "[The teachers of the law] devour widows' houses and for a show make lengthy prayers. These men will be punished most severely" (11:47^{NIV}). Jesus's praise of the widow's sacrificial giving is in the direct context of his condemnation of wealthy religious leaders who had put the widows out on the streets in the first place.

Another famous example is Jesus praising the faith of sex workers who trusted in the message of the kin(g)dom of God. In response to the chief priests and elders of Israel challenging his authority, Jesus said, "Truly I tell you, the tax collectors and the prostitutes are entering the kingdom of God ahead of you. For John came to you to show you the way of righteousness, and you did not believe him, but the tax collectors and the prostitutes did. And even after you saw this, you did not repent and believe him" (Matthew 21:31b–32NIV).

But perhaps most interesting of all is the way Jesus centers eunuchs in an extended dialogue with Pharisees about the kingdom of heaven in Matthew 19. In the midst of a fascinating discussion of divorce, Jesus's disciples say, "If this is the situation between a husband and wife, it is better not to marry" (Matthew 19:10). Jesus then responds by saying,

> *Not everyone can accept this word, but only those to whom it has been given. For there are eunuchs who were born that way, and there are eunuchs who have been made eunuchs by others—and there are those who choose to live like eunuchs for the sake of the kingdom of heaven. The one who can accept this should accept it.* (Matthew 19:11–12NIV)

Much like Jesus's centering of the Samaritan in one of his most famous parables, the centering of eunuchs here is no accident. Like John before him, Jesus too has chosen a life of singleness due to his full devotion to God's kin(g)dom. By comparing himself to a eunuch, Jesus demonstrates the striking social reversal his kin(g)dom brings. Eunuchs were a marginalized group, whether they were born that way or made that way by others. They didn't fit into a society like the one Jesus lived in that prized building one's social standing and legacy on one's family. Eunuchs weren't considered male any longer, but also weren't considered female.[1] In this sense, they occupied a liminal space in relation to gender and gender roles, and patriarchal societies marginalize people and groups that don't fit neatly into assigned gender roles. Here Jesus identifies with a marginalized group that doesn't conform to societal norms of gender, sexuality, and marriage.

In fact, Jesus explicitly identifies with marginalized social groups a few chapters later when he teaches on how God judges faithfulness. Jesus says he accepts as service to him, service given to people who lack food, clothing, or who are sick. He says he also accepts as service to him, service given to strangers and prisoners. "Truly I tell you, whatever you did for one of the least of these brothers and sisters of mine, you did for me" (Matthew 25:40).

Jesus's social reversal of insiders and outsiders revolutionizes our notions of what makes a person fit for God's kin(g)dom. People aren't fit for God's kin(g)dom simply because they are suited to accepted social norms. Quite the opposite! The ones Jesus calls into his kin(g)dom are the misfits and the marginalized.

X-MEN VERSUS *GUARDIANS OF THE GALAXY*

I learned a lot about being a misfit from comic books. Long before the *Marvel Cinematic Universe/Multiverse* became such a mainstream movie juggernaut, I loved *Spiderman* and *Fantastic Four* comics. But I especially loved *X-Men* comics. Something about the lore of mutants resonated deeply with me, as I know it does with many teenagers. Maybe it's the feeling that there's something about you that's different from others, the feeling of going through changes that others don't understand. In *X-Men* comics, young adults often discover they have superhuman abilities due to a sudden crisis or a particularly stressful experience. This catalytic event would launch characters into a spiral of mental distress and social isolation. If they revealed their new powers to others, even family, those others would often become so afraid they would react in violent ways. Parents rejected their own children. Government officials enacted policies to protect society from these strange and dangerous teens. I'm not the first to note how closely this parallels the experience of so many LGBTQ+ youth. Like the mutants in the *X-Men* comics, LGBTQ+ youth have learned to keep discoveries about themselves a secret and trust no one. In the comics, this turned the mutants into outcasts. But then came Professor X.

Charles Xavier, also known as Professor X, himself a powerful mutant, formed a school for "gifted youngsters" that was a safe haven for mutants. At this school, young mutants would learn how to harness their frightening powers and turn them into gifts that could be used for the good of all humanity. In fact, at the center of the school was a team of those who had achieved this success: the *X-Men*. They were each powerfully gifted mutants, superheroes in their own right. But when they came together they were even more powerful. Mutants such as Storm, Jean Grey, Cyclops, and Wolverine formed the core of this team. Storm could control the weather and command lightning. Cyclops could blast a powerful beam from his eyes. All on their own, they were powerful and heroic. But they chose to operate as a team, with Professor X as their leader, and use their gifts to complement one another.

When I came to faith as a teenager and began to follow Jesus as his disciple, I was drawn to the analogy of the body of Christ functioning like the *X-Men*. In fact, after I'd discerned a calling into vocational ministry and began to practice preaching, this was the subject of one of my very first sermons. It helped that I came to faith through the Pentecostal tradition, in which a lot of emphasis is placed on gifts of the Holy Spirit. We focused a lot of attention on 1 Corinthians—especially the parts about spiritual gifts. In that context, Paul was teaching the church how to live as a new kind of family, one with a common unity. Paul says that the Holy Spirit distributes gifts to every member of the body of Christ and that each member is necessary, just like the *X-Men*. So, some of my earliest thoughts about what it means to be a healthy community were shaped both by scripture and superheroes. I envisioned the "perfect" community of Jesus-disciples to be just like the *X-Men*—each member was a superhero in their own right. Each member had a powerful gift and could fight their own battles. Of course, we'd be even more powerful together. But, essentially, we were all self-sufficient superhumans.

Then in 2014, one comic I hadn't read as a teen was made into a movie: *Guardians of the Galaxy*. This was a much different take on the superhero team than the *X-Men*, even though there was a lot of overlap. On both teams, each member had special abilities, sometimes even superhuman powers. On both teams, the members worked together to overcome enemies. But there was one significant factor that set the *Guardians of the Galaxy* apart from the *X-Men*: The *Guardians of the Galaxy* were misfits, deliberately cast as outsiders, cultural nonconformists. While the *X-Men* could often blend in to the broader society by simply not wearing their signature matching uniforms, the *Guardians of the Galaxy* were brazenly conspicuous. One of the *Guardians of the Galaxy* is a huge tree, for example, and another is a talking raccoon. One has antennae and two have green skin!

But there's something even more basically different about these two teams. In the 2014 *Guardians of the Galaxy* movie, each member of the team has a tragic backstory that has left them emotionally (and often physically) scarred. On their own, they often tend toward self-destructive behaviors. They are haunted by the ghosts of their past, or they are desperate to find out who they really are. Only when they find one another, and form a new kind of family for one another, do they begin their healing journeys. While the mutants in the *X-Men* comics were often ostracized and cast out of their respective families, by the time they joined together to form a team, they had achieved some level of stability and mastery of themselves. By contrast, the *Guardians of the Galaxy* depended on one another to maintain their trajectory toward self-mastery.

The longer I've been a disciple of Jesus, and especially the longer I've served as a pastor, the more I see the body of Christ as a *Guardians of the Galaxy* type of community rather than an *X-Men* kind of community. It seems like a superhero like Storm could do without the rest of the *X-Men*, but a superhero like Drax couldn't. It seems like the *X-Men* are a loose association of superheroes more than an interdependent family on a healing journey together. And the *X-Men* seem like they have it more "together" than the *Guardians of the Galaxy*, who are still figuring themselves out. That's been more my experience as a pastor and a follower of Jesus. Followers of Jesus form a new kind of family—the kind that needs one another and encourages one another as we all journey together toward healing and wholeness. We don't have it all together, but we have one another. And often it's those who think they have it all together who are the most oblivious to their need for others in community. Perhaps even more to the point, it's often those who are most marginalized by the broader society who reveal the true beauty of inclusive community.

TONY AND "THE HOMELESS"

When I began serving as a pastor in downtown Los Angeles, I knew next to nothing about Skid Row. Just from the name alone I assumed it was a single street that had a disproportionate population of unhoused persons. But after a long-time resident of Skid Row and church member gave me a "tour," I learned it's actually a large neighborhood with many businesses and nonprofits. Blocks and blocks of streets with tents lining each sidewalk are directly adjacent to luxury high-rise apartments. It never ceased to amaze me when I would routinely see Lamborghinis and Ferraris parked mere blocks from people living on sidewalks. Pastoring in such close proximity to Skid Row deepened my commitment to addressing structural inequality in society, and it confronted me with my own unconscious bias against people experiencing homelessness.

Tony was a young man who attended our church and lived on the street due to severely strained relationships with his biological family and untreated mental illness. During the day, he would often come and hang out in our church offices where he could get out of the heat and have someone to talk to, which often meant me. This was really challenging for me at first. I initially felt annoyed by Tony and just wanted him to leave me alone. Didn't he know I had paperwork to do, or sermons to write? Couldn't he see that I was busy? But, Tony was also joyful and inquisitive. When I wasn't consumed by my to-do list, I found that I really enjoyed talking with him. Tony wasn't a fully stable, self-sufficient superhuman, but then again neither was I. Tony hadn't reached the end of his journey of self-discovery and self-mastery, but neither had I really. Tony and I weren't as different as I'd initially thought.

Slowly, as the Spirit worked on me, I began to think of Tony as less of a liability and more of an asset to our community. When I asked him if he'd like to help out around the office, he jumped at the opportunity. And as we explored together some of the ways he could contribute, I discovered that Tony was actually a quite gifted visual artist. He was entirely self-taught, but his graffiti style was very advanced. He created signs and other visual art for the office that gave it a uniquely LA style. And our relationship produced much more than decorations; it produced trust and mutual understanding. I got to know more about why he was living on the street and the ways the community could support him. We ended up spending a lot of time together and helped him overcome some fears that were preventing him from getting help. Tony is just one example of the many unhoused members of that church who became spiritual family.

And yet, every Sunday after the worship gathering had concluded, I would stand in the lobby under a red tent and field questions from visitors. Due to our obvious socioeconomic diversity and our proximity to Skid Row, one of the most common questions I'd receive is, "How does this church serve the homeless?" The first year or so, I tried to answer the question with the kinds of programs we supported or our connection to shelters in Skid Row. But, eventually, I saw this question as fundamentally misguided. "The homeless" were not some group of people who are separate from our church; our fellowship was made up of people, some of whom are housed and some of whom are unhoused. Tony isn't "the homeless." Tony is my brother in Christ and a member of this community. Service isn't a one-way street; we serve one another. Tony serves his community, and his community serves him. Having to answer this question from new visitors over and over each week helped solidify my perspective on what it means to be the body of Christ. Rather than viewing Jesus communities as loose associations of superhuman individuals, I was reminded that Jesus called us together to become an interdependent family on a journey toward healing and wholeness.

GIVING SPECIAL HONOR

Jesus said that his disciples were joined to him in a "new covenant"—a renewed relationship between humanity and God through him (Luke 22:20). That same covenant is what bonds us to one another in a new kind of family forged by the Spirit. This new covenant family has a common unity, *community*, constituted by our mutual interdependence and our shared identity in the Messiah. To illuminate this, the apostle Paul uses the analogy that was common in his day of a society functioning like a body. However, Paul flips the typical use of this analogy on its head.

In the Greco-Roman culture in which Paul was immersed, the body analogy was used to suggest that some groups in society were destined to be functionally subordinate to other groups. The "feet" of society were the laborers and smiths, farmers and fishermen. But the "head" of society were the politicians and philosophers, along with the aristocracy. This analogy was employed to keep everyone in their place, so to speak. But Paul completely subverts this notion by drawing more deeply on the bodily analogy. In actuality, the parts of a body are all biologically interconnected. A head can't walk without the rest of the body, particularly the feet. So the notion that the body analogy could ascribe subordination to one part under another violates the way a physical body actually operates.

> *Just as a body, though one, has many parts, but all its many parts form one body, so it is with Christ. For we were all baptized by one Spirit so as to form one body—whether Jews or Gentiles, slave or free—and we were all given the one Spirit to drink. Even so the body is not made up of one part but of many.* (1 Corinthians 12:12–14[NIV])

The members of the body Paul is talking about aren't individuals, they're groups. Where sin-riddled society (the world gone wrong) has created divisions, the Spirit creates unity. While in the broader society, ethnicity and gender are dividing walls, in the body of Christ they're reimagined as complementary gifts. Each part of the body has an indispensable role to play. And where there has been inequality in society due to injustice, in the body of Christ the *shalom*-bringing Spirit corrects those imbalances.

In the early church, slaves were baptized into the same fellowship as free persons and treated as equal siblings. While they may be assigned a lower social status outside the assembly of disciples, in the fellowship of the Messiah no such stigma is allowed. While the world gone wrong believes it is natural for some people to own other people, in the body of Christ, the Spirit rejects such hierarchy because all human beings are made in God's image and are worth Christ dying on the Cross ("brother or sister, for whom Christ died," 1 Corinthians 8:11[NIV]). Elevating slaves to equal honor in the church was a radical and subversive act that disrupted the Roman social system (i.e., the *pater familias*). It challenged the very foundations of their beliefs about human nature and what it means to have a healthy, functioning society.

Women were also elevated in the early church. Paul routinely names women as his colaborers in the calling of preaching the gospel and shepherding God's flock. He names some as leaders of house churches, like Priscilla, and others he calls apostles, like Junia. And he gave Phoebe the role of literally preaching his letter to the church in Rome. Despite what some Christian groups today believe, Paul was radical in his inclusion and honoring of women for a first-century Jewish man—and that was because he was a disciple of Jesus, who had honored and elevated women throughout his ministry.

Furthermore, in the first century Jews were despised by Gentiles, such as Greeks and Romans, for their idiosyncratic worship practices, like kosher eating and sabbath-keeping, their impiety (having only one God), and their exclusiveness (e.g., circumcision). But Jews also despised Gentiles because they were "unclean" and pagans, worshipping many gods. There was power imbalance in Roman society: Gentiles were the dominant culture. But, in the church, there was a reverse power imbalance: Jews were the gatekeepers of the faith. In Paul's letter to the Corinthians, he is teaching them that the Jesus Way corrects those imbalances and destroys those divisions by uniting our diverse identities in the Messiah. Because we have been baptized into the faith of Jesus and been filled with his Spirit, our identities are no longer governed by those power imbalances. In direct contrast, the body of Christ honors those who are dishonored and uplifts those who are downtrodden, so there can be mutuality and equity.

The eye cannot say to the hand, "I don't need you!" And the head cannot say to the feet, "I don't need you!" On the contrary, those parts of the body that seem to be weaker are indispensable, and the parts that we think are less honorable we treat with special honor. And the parts that are unpresentable are treated with special modesty, while our presentable parts need no special treatment. But God has put the body together, giving greater honor to the parts that lacked it, so that there should be no division in the body, but that its parts should have equal concern for each other. If one part suffers, every part suffers with it; if one part is honored, every part rejoices with it. (1 Corinthians 12:21–26[NIV])

The way that Jesus forges a new kind of family is by creating a microcosm of the *shalom* (i.e., wholeness, harmony, justice, etc.) that will one day characterize the restored world. Injustices that divide people, advantaging some at the expense of others, are rectified. Divisions that have been socially constructed based on the way people look or cultural customs are eliminated. Every people and language group is celebrated as a beautiful reflection of the divine image. This future restoration begins in seed form among the followers of Jesus. We are gathered as a contrast community, subverting norms that marginalize, and honoring those who are socially dishonored. We pay special attention to those whom Jesus paid special attention. We see them as Jesus saw them. Revolutionaries and tax collectors were thought of as less honorable. So Jesus treated them with special honor. Sex workers and the disabled were thought of as unpresentable. So Jesus treated them with special modesty. Social stigmas of "weakness" are replaced by indispensable value. This is the Jesus Way!

LEVERAGING PRIVILEGE

Paul says those groups that are already perceived to be "presentable" in the broader society "need no special treatment" among the community of Jesus disciples. They are unjustly advantaged. Paul prescribes a countermeasure: greater honor is given to the groups that "lack it" in the wider world.

Today, in American society, the LGBTQ+ community is marginalized and singled out for draconian policies and legislation. Black, Latino/a, Native American, and Asian communities continue to suffer due to racism. Women continue to be objectified and harassed, undervalued, and their bodies controlled. Therefore, it's incumbent upon followers of Jesus with social privilege to use all available means to rectify these injustices both in the family of God and in society at large.

For me, this has meant repenting of the ways I've participated in gatekeeping power in the church and using every means available to me to advocate for greater equity. This requires me to renounce theologies that deny my LGBTQ+ siblings access to leadership, full participation, and blessed marriages. It's my work to interrogate ways that "welcome" hasn't meant "full inclusion." Likewise, predominately White spaces have often purported to welcome diversity but have done little or nothing to seek justice for Black and Brown bodies, to oppose their brutalization, or to redress systemic racism. Leveraging my privilege as a White male has meant speaking out and standing up to other White males who remain defensive and protective of the status quo. Forging family in the way of Jesus has meant deconstructing systems of power in the church and embracing a posture of humility and empathy toward those with marginalized identities. It has required confession and repentance, death and resurrection. In short, it has meant loving others the way Jesus has loved me. The result is a community in which every member is treated with God-honoring dignity, celebrated as a child of God, and united in a new kind of family.

Another important way that family is forged in the way of Jesus is by confronting power dynamics that harm and repairing them. This requires those who have been afforded unjust advantages to reckon within themselves with the fear of losing power and privilege. This is another refining fire. Forging family in the way of Jesus requires a new kind of commitment to one another: a covenant one. But to understand what covenanting with one another means, we will have to reexamine our understanding of grace.

9 | REDEEMING GRACE

A new command I give you: Love one another.
As I have loved you, so you must love one another.

John 13:34^{NIV}

THE "LOVE BANK"

When Osheta and I were newly married, we attended a marriage conference in Rhode Island. Truth be told, we were much more excited by the prospect of having a weekend away from our young kids to just be together in the picturesque New England city of Newport than we were about the conference itself. But we did our best to absorb at least some of the content we were taught.

My biggest take away from that conference, however, was an interaction I had with one of the conference leaders in a breakout session just for the husbands. The way I remember it, this teacher, who had been married for several decades, was teaching with a posture of "let me share with you the real secret to marriage— the inside scoop." Then he proceeded to use the analogy of a "love bank." He said something that amounted to, "Your marriage has a love bank, and if you're having problems, it's likely because you're trying to make withdrawals from the 'love bank,' but your request is coming back 'insufficient funds.' If you want to be able to make a withdrawal from the 'love bank,' you've got to make sure you've been making deposits."

Now, I'm a naturally curious and skeptical person, and at this point I was first- or second-year seminary student, which means I was possibly at my most argumentative. This "love bank" teaching wasn't sitting right with me at all. My hand shot up, and I held it there until he acknowledged me.

I said, "That's not how God's grace works. God's grace is *unmerited favor*. If God is our model of how relationships and love are supposed to work, why is it that in marriage love is earned through deposits in a 'love bank'?"

His response was something like, "Well God's grace is different from your wife's grace."

You can probably already guess that I was less than satisfied by his answer. But what I came to realize much later is that the teacher wasn't necessarily wrong about marriage. Now that I've been married for twenty years, I can attest to the wisdom of his "love bank" analogy. What was wrong was my understanding of *grace*—an understanding that is deeply indebted to modern Western notions. Allow me to explain.

GRACE MEANS GIFT

Modern Western culture has distorted our picture of grace from what is taught in the New Testament. It starts with the very language we use. Unlike modern English, the words that Paul uses in the New Testament that are translated as "grace" are generic, everyday words for gift, favor, or benefit. They weren't special religious words. In the West, we often use "gift" generically and "grace" religiously. But there was no such distinction for Paul or the other authors of the New Testament. The Greek word *charis* is often rendered "grace" in many modern English translations. But Paul also mixes this term with other typical and nonspecialized words for gift like *dōrea*, *dōrmea*, and *charisma* in the same context. For example, in Romans chapter 5, Paul uses all four of these terms in the same thought to describe the gift of Jesus's saving life.[1] This means that terms we've come to think of in exclusively religious ways are subject to everyday cultural norms of giving and receiving gifts. And cultural norms around giving and receiving gifts are highly contextual. Modern Western norms are very different from ancient Eastern norms.

In fact, one of the most important cultural factors related to gifts is the question of who is worthy to receive one. In the ancient context in which the New Testament was written—the Greco-Roman world and the Jewish community within it—gifts were thought to be best given to those who were deemed worthy to receive them. Just like in much of the world today, for the ancient cultures of Jesus and Paul, to give a gift to someone who was part of a group that was deemed dishonorable by societal norms would lower the giver's social standing. The very act of giving someone a gift ties the giver to the recipient in a social relationship. Not to mention, the giving of significant gifts to those who aren't thought to be worthy of them would be considered a waste. This way of viewing worthiness for receiving a gift isn't all that difficult to understand from a modern, Western standpoint. All we have to do is think about one of the most famous gift-givers in modern Western culture—the jolly old elf himself: Santa Claus.

WHO IS WORTHY?

Westerners know that Santa exercises discretion about whom he gifts; he has a "nice list." Only deserving children whose behavior has merited a reward are given presents on Christmas. With this cultural framework running unconsciously in the background of our minds, we will inevitably evaluate the worthiness of those whom we think deserve to receive grace. We could even be unconsciously influenced by the culture around us to put entire groups of people on our "worthy" or "unworthy" lists. "Those people," (whoever "those people" happen to be) "aren't *worthy* of grace," we are tempted to think.

Some traditions, perhaps most notably the Reformed or Calvinist tradition, are convinced they've solved this problem: No one is worthy! In fact, some of the most famous preachers in American history gained their notoriety in part for how persuasively they communicated the unworthiness of human beings for God's grace. Jonathan Edwards comes to mind. His infamous sermon, "Sinners in the Hands of an Angry God," contains this passage: "The God that holds you over the Pit of Hell, much as one holds a Spider, or some loathsome Insect, over the Fire, abhors you, and is dreadfully provoked; his Wrath towards you burns like Fire; he looks upon you as worthy of nothing else, but to be cast into the Fire; he is of purer Eyes than to bear to have you in his Sight; you are ten thousand Times so abominable in his Eyes as the most hateful venomous Serpent is in ours."[2] Or, more recently, Calvinist pastor Mark Driscoll became famous in part for how boldly he pronounced the unworthiness of human beings to receive God's grace.[3] Because of these pastors' widespread fame and seeming commitment to the Bible, it may come as a surprise to learn that not only is such teaching psychologically damaging, it's also not what the New Testament teaches.

Rather than teaching that only some receive God's grace because none are worthy, the New Testament teaches that God gives the gracious gift of Jesus Christ and salvation to the entire world because of God's gracious nature. God's grace has been poured out not because of humanity's worthiness or unworthiness, but because God loves the world. "For God so loved the world that he gave his one and only Son, that whoever believes in him shall not perish but have eternal life" (John 3:16[NIV]). God gives because God loves. In fact, God's gracious gift of Jesus Christ reveals God's gracious nature unlike anything else. "The Word became flesh and made his dwelling among us. We have seen his glory, the glory of the One and Only, who came from the Father, full of grace and truth. . . . No one has ever seen God, but God the One and Only, who is at the Father's side, has made him known" (John 1:14, 18[NIV]). So the grace of God is the revelation of God's graciousness, not our worthiness or unworthiness.

But there's more. Once Jesus has decided to give himself as a gift to the whole world, this grace *makes* us worthy. Not only are we divine image-bearers—God's representative stewards of the earth—we are now divine image-bearers "for whom Christ died"

(Romans 14:15; 1 Corinthians 8:11). The apostle Paul wrote to the Jesus communities in first-century Rome and Corinth to say, honor one another and bear with one another because the people with whom you are in community are people for whom the Messiah died. *God's grace ennobles us!* God's grace doesn't go looking for people who are good enough to receive it—like Santa's "nice" list. No, God's grace *confers* worth upon us without preconditions. In Ephesians, Jesus disciples are urged to live lives worthy of the grace they have *already* received—not that they have been worthy to receive (4:1).

God's grace isn't like receiving a free car on *The Price is Right*. God's grace is more like receiving a car before we've learned how to drive, along with a driving instructor, and someplace that we're called to drive. That way, we want to learn how to drive so that we can get to the destination in the new car that we've been so generously given. Rather than being based on the recipient's driving ability, the purpose of the gift and how to use it are included in the gift. Contrary to modern Western notions of the perfect gift, there are "strings attached."

NO STRINGS ATTACHED?

If modern Western culture has taught us anything about grace, it's that grace is *free*. But what does that mean? Does it simply mean that the recipient didn't "earn" the gift, so that it isn't confused for compensation? Or does it also entail the idea that there are "no strings attached"? Everyone knows Santa doesn't have demands about how children play with the toys they are given. And everyone knows that Santa doesn't expect a gift in return. The modern Western notion of grace is one-directional.

But for the vast majority of human history—including the time of Jesus and Paul—and for the vast majority of cultures around the globe today, *reciprocity* in gift-giving was and is the norm. The idea that the perfect gift is one that is given unconditionally is an extremely novel and minority view. In particular, this was not the cultural assumption of Greeks, Romans, or Jews in the first century. Ancient and Eastern peoples like Jesus and the apostle Paul assumed that gift-giving not only entailed obligations of some kind, but also established or maintained a relationship. So even though God's grace is not conditioned upon some preexisting worthiness, that doesn't mean God's grace comes without expectations.

As difficult as it may be for Americans to accept, Paul wrote to some Jesus communities about the debt they owed because of God's grace. Paul didn't view grace as *free* as much as *costly*. Like when Paul was writing about "the collection," he was eager to "remember the poor," as he was reminded by Peter, James, and John in Jerusalem. This meant that as he began forming Jesus communities among the Greeks and Romans, he would raise funds for the mostly Jewish Jesus-disciples back in Jerusalem who were suffering. Today, we would expect Paul to appeal to these Gentiles for *charity*, but Paul doesn't. Instead, he writes, "Now, however, I am on my way to Jerusalem in the service of the Lord's people there. For Macedonia and Achaia were pleased to make a contribution for the poor among the Lord's people in Jerusalem. They were pleased to do it, and indeed they owe it to them. For if the Gentiles have shared in the Jews' spiritual blessings, they owe it to the Jews to share with them their material blessings" (Romans 15:25–27 NIV). For Paul, the generosity of the Gentile Jesus communities wasn't pure altruism, it was an expected part of being united with their Jewish siblings in the family of Jesus.

I didn't begin to understand the connection between a distorted view of grace and distorted views of community development until I was in seminary in Boston. There I began serving in various community development ministries, including one called the Emmanuel Gospel Center, or EGC. The leaders at EGC were seasoned veterans of urban ministry. They had decades of experience, tons of advanced degrees, and time-tested godly wisdom.

One day I was talking to one of EGC's leaders named Ruth Wong about urban ministry strategy. I was asking her about how to get more of the resourced churches in the suburbs to give to ministries and churches in the urban core that are struggling financially. In my mind, what needed to happen was that the wealthy suburban churches that were building brand new multimillion dollar campuses needed to give a portion of their annual budgets to the ministries and churches in the urban core who could hardly afford to pay their pastors. She said that what was desperately needed in the relationships between urban and suburban communities was not generosity but *reciprocity*. I was so confused. How on earth would churches in the urban core that were financially strapped give to churches in the wealthy Boston suburbs that didn't need it? But she helped me to see that money wasn't the only needed resource. Urban churches had so much more to offer that suburban churches needed. I think that's what Paul was talking about when he wrote,

"Our desire is not that others might be relieved while you are hard pressed, but that there might be equality. At the present time your plenty will supply what they need, so that in turn their plenty will supply what you need. The goal is equality, as it is written: 'The one who gathered much did not have too much, and the one who gathered little did not have too little'" (2 Corinthians 8:13–15 ᴺᴵⱽ).

Paul's concern here is for mutuality, the sharing of resources with those in need. His theology of giving is very different from the modern concept of charity. Paul doesn't view the contributions of the Gentile Jesus communities to their Jewish siblings as unconditional or unmerited. On the contrary, reciprocity in their relationship is a byproduct of their unity that's been forged in the Messiah and part of a relational debt owed.

In the New Testament, God's grace establishes a new kind of relationship with humanity—a new *covenant*. A covenant is a sacred agreement that binds parties to one another for a purpose. A covenant absolutely entails expectations, even obligations. So, while God's grace can certainly be thought of as *unconditioned*— not dependent on preexisting worthiness—it's not *unconditional*. For the German theologian and martyr Dietrich Bonhoeffer, such an unconditional view of God's grace was at the root of the rise of Nazism in the German Lutheran church. He wrote, "Cheap grace is preaching forgiveness without repentance; it is baptism without the discipline of community; it is the Lord's Supper without confession of sin; it is absolution without personal confession. Cheap grace is grace without discipleship, grace without the cross, grace without the living, incarnate Jesus Christ."[4] Without a covenant relationship with God, and all that such a covenant entails, "unconditional grace" papers over our responsibilities to God and one another.

One of the primary passages where we can look for the New Testament's theology of grace is Ephesians 2:1–22. If we were to stop reading at Ephesians 2, verses 1 through 10, we might be tempted to read into these verses about God's grace an unconditional tone. But if we continue reading through verse 11 all the way to verse 22, we see that God's grace establishes a reality: one new humanity—a united community that includes people of different ethnic and cultural heritages. This new, covenant community is bonded to one another not by their blood but by Christ's blood. They are a new kind of family: "you are no longer foreigners and strangers, but fellow citizens with God's people and also members of his household."

This is what I experienced when I was sixteen and encountered the grace of God through the power of the Holy Spirit. I wasn't written a blank check or handed a golden ticket to heaven. No, I was invited into a new multiethnic and culturally-inclusive family and shown that I belonged in that family and had a role to play.

UNCLE BLAKE AND AUNT DEBBIE

When Osheta and I were living in Los Angeles and I was serving as a pastor in downtown LA, we were struggling in many ways—feeling beaten down and depleted. A couple in our church named Blake and Debbie Waltman who cared about us offered to watch our kids for us and send us to a resort and spa in San Luis Obispo. Every cabin had a natural spring hot tub, and it was a short walk from the beach. It was the most relaxing and extravagant gift Osheta or I had ever been given.

I think receiving a gift like that does something to a person. It changed my view of myself. I was forced to view myself as a person who has been deemed worthy of being given such a gift. It made me want to be the kind of person who is worthy of such a gift. Even more than that, it made Blake and Debbie family. We were broke urban ministers, so we couldn't reciprocate with anything close to an in-kind gift. But they didn't *want* anything material in return. They wanted to be part of our lives. That's how Blake and Debbie became *Uncle* Blake and *Aunt* Debbie.

That's a picture of God's grace. In Jesus, God has conferred upon us the most extravagant gift imaginable—a gift we could never even come close to repaying. But God doesn't want repayment. God wants to forge a new kind of family with us, a covenant family. God wants to empower us to become the human beings we are meant to be. That's how the grace of God works.

We in the West have often misunderstood grace because we've conceptualized it as a one-way, unilateral donation. But God's grace doesn't actually work that way. God is not obligated by some external force to provide grace. That much is true. Rather, God provides grace because God is essentially gracious. What's untrue is that God's grace is unconditional. God's grace is *unconditioned*, but not *unconditional*. God's provision of grace creates a relational bond, a covenanted family. And God's grace isn't charity; covenant entails expectations. God's grace establishes a relationship that has very clear stipulations and obligations. God is forging people into a new kind of family.

10 | COMMUNITY OF MISFITS

Then Jesus said to his host, "When you give a luncheon or dinner, do not invite your friends, your brothers or sisters, your relatives, or your rich neighbors; if you do, they may invite you back and so you will be repaid.

But when you give a banquet, invite the poor, the crippled, the lame, the blind, and you will be blessed. Although they cannot repay you, you will be repaid at the resurrection of the righteous."

Luke 14:12–14^{NIV}

REPLANTING ROOTS

"If we ever accept another call, the next place we live has to be somewhere we can set down roots," Osheta said with finality, and I whole-heartedly agreed. At this point, we'd already followed God's call to move cross-country twice: from New Orleans to Boston and from Boston to LA. We both felt like our next move had to be someplace where we could finish raising our kids and launch them into adulthood.

She also said this on the heels of one of the most devastating disappointments of my life. In LA, I'd suffered verbal and emotional abuse from a pastor I served with, a pastor who wielded all the power over the church's board. So, ultimately, he was able to force me to resign even though I was the one harmed. As traumatizing as that was, it still wasn't my breaking point. After my resignation, a beloved mentor recommended me to be the pastor of a church he planted in Washington, DC—a church we saw as well-aligned with our family's values of peace-making and racial justice. They sent elders to LA to interview me and hear me preach. We hosted one of the elders in our home, and our whole family played board games together. We have a family tradition of writing the name of each game's winner on the inside of the game's box lid with a tally as we all chant, "Name in the box! Name in the box!" We gladly added the visiting elder's name to our family's box lid when she won. After all, she was family too.

The church's pastoral search committee narrowed the field to two candidates in the final stage of the weeks-long and nerve-racking process. This truly felt like my last chance at ministry. If this fell through, I didn't see a future on the other side—and that's unlike me. An elder called with their decision. They'd decided to go with the other candidate. I was destroyed. I hung up the phone and collapsed onto our bed. It was the end, I thought. Maybe I could go back into graphic design. Maybe I could go back to school for social work and forget about local church ministry. It was about as close to an identity crisis as I'd had since becoming a follower of Jesus as a teenager. There just didn't seem to be any hope that we'd ever find the kind of community that was right for us.

"If I'm ever going to pastor again, it would have to be a church that already has some established leadership and infrastructure," I remember saying. "I don't think I can start from scratch again. I'm just too tired now."

"And it has to be in a city with lower cost of living, so we're not struggling again just to make it while pastoring," Osheta wisely said.

"It also has to be an urban and multiethnic congregation." It was 2017, and churches across the country were in the grip of deep polarization because of fissures exacerbated by the Trump administration. I was deeply afraid of how painful it would be to once again move our family to a new city, embed them in a new community, only to face accusations of playing politics from some misinformed members of the congregation who don't understand Jesus's vision for *shalom*.

"It also has to be a church that is part of a denomination too. I won't ever serve another 'non-denominational' church again. There has to be accountability." We'd already had this conviction before we moved to LA, but we'd compromised and learned the hard way. Never again.

The list kept growing. By now, the odds seemed astronomical. Finding the right community of faith isn't just difficult for pastors, it's difficult for all of us. We have a long list of criteria in our heads, and it becomes easy to believe that no such community exists.

At this time, we'd begun worshipping with a precious Mennonite congregation in Pasadena, and Osheta had asked people to pray for us. But our hopes were fading fast. Uncle Blake and

Aunt Debbie called to encourage us. They said we could always come to Spokane and live with them until we got back on our feet. We were seriously considering it.

A few weeks later, someone from Osheta's book launch team reached out to her. Osheta had asked her launch team to pray for us as we discerned our next move, and this woman had just visited a church she thought might be a good fit for us and that Sunday they announced they were beginning a pastoral search. The name of the church was Roots, and it was in Saint Paul, Minnesota.

ALWAYS TOO MUCH OR NOT ENOUGH

Osheta and I were surprised to learn that Roots was looking for a pastor because we'd met the pastor who planted Roots, Touger Thao, years before at a church-planting conference in Florida. We were fascinated to learn more about both Touger and his wife Mykou, their story as Hmong Americans living in Minnesota, and about their vision for a new kind of church.

"It's so cool that you're planting a Hmong church!" I naively said to him.

"I'm not. I'm planting an intentionally multiethnic church. A church for anyone who feels like a misfit," Touger said.

"Oh! I love that!" I said, embarrassed by my assumption.

As is common with many immigrant and refugee communities throughout the United States, first- and second-generation Hmong Americans in Minnesota often describe feeling like they're caught between two worlds, not "Hmong enough" but also not

"American enough." Touger and Mykou planted Roots not only for those who felt this way because of their ethnic and cultural identities, but also for those who felt like misfits for other reasons. Some members of the original launch team said they didn't feel "religious enough" for church or they felt like they didn't fit within the political landscape at the time. Roots was planted as a "community of misfits, finding identity in Jesus." It was created for people with complex identities—people who don't fit neatly into the prescribed boxes.

And that's a big part of what drew us to Roots. Osheta and I have often felt like misfits in many of the Christian spaces we've occupied—always too much or not enough. We've been the ones who asked too many questions or didn't fully conform to established cultural norms. But the idea of a community that carves out a space for people like us gave us hope. We heard ourselves saying things like, "Maybe Roots could be the kind of community we always dreamed of, the kind that's truly Jesus-centered and makes room for everyone."

So we flew to Saint Paul and met with these Minnesota misfits. We went bowling, we attended a costume party for Halloween, and we had a lot of conversations with people who were part of Roots. What we heard over and over was so encouraging. They said they didn't think of themselves as very religious and typically weren't regular church-goers, but that Roots was different. Roots was more than just a Sunday morning worship gathering, it was a community. They said that they'd never felt so free to be themselves, to question and explore faith, and they'd never learned as much about other people and their faith. By making space for "misfits," Roots was helping people heal and grow.

Back in LA, we waited as Roots voted whether to call me as their pastor. It was a stressful time, but by this point we were confident this was where God was calling us, and we were right. Roots voted overwhelmingly to call me as their pastor. However, this didn't make the transition from LA to Minnesota completely seamless. In the process of finalizing the logistics of moving to Saint Paul and signing the pastoral contract, we discovered that there were a couple people with influence left in the church who were opposed to Roots having any pastor at all. In the intervening year between when Touger had stepped down and I had been called, a few people had stepped in to fill the leadership vacuum, and at least one of them didn't want to step aside. When my contract was held up without explanation, we quickly learned who was the one who didn't want us there. It was beginning to feel like we were too much or not enough even for this community of misfits.

There's a lesson in this part of our journey for all of us. Even when we are operating in our callings, even when we've submitted ourselves to the Spirit and a thorough discernment process, we may still face challenges and opposition to our destinies. Be prepared! Forging family in the way of Jesus is never a walk in the park.

Eventually, excruciatingly, the details were finalized, and we began yet another cross-country adventure to a new city, this time with the hope of setting down roots. But the move still wasn't entirely painless. Osheta and I were wounded when the person who didn't want Roots to have a pastor said and did hurtful things to us. After a church-wide retreat in our new home, for example, she cornered Osheta in our kitchen and told her that she'd held up my contract because she felt Roots needed to be protected from us. Despite receiving a 97 percent approving vote to call me as their pastor, this woman felt she knew what was best for Roots. She would go on to leave the church not long after, but the leaders who stayed formed a team with us, rallied around us, and encouraged us. Even though they'd held the church together for nearly a year without a pastor, they continued to serve until a new leadership team could be elected. This kind of sacrificial service convinced us that we weren't too much or not enough for Roots, but that Roots was after all a community that could hold even our misfit-ness.

CHOSEN MISFITS

Mark's Gospel says that Jesus didn't just proclaim the kin(g)dom of God, he began demonstrating it by gathering to himself apprentices, the first members of this new kind of family. The first place we see him call people into his family is along the Sea of Galilee. Jesus saw two common fishermen, Simon and Andrew, casting their nets into the lake, and he called to them, "Come, follow me, and I will send you out to fish for people" (Mark 1:17^{NIV}). Likewise, Jesus gathered James and his brother John from their fishing boats. Later in Mark, Jesus calls a man named Levi to be his disciple while Levi was still sitting in his tax collector's booth (2:14). Later still, Mark records a list of the disciples Jesus called to himself that includes "Simon the Zealot" (3:18).

Jesus didn't go to Jerusalem to find the most promising young rabbis, gifted scholars, or accomplished scribes. Jesus didn't go to Qumran where there was an extremely devout community of Jews awaiting the Messiah. Jesus didn't choose the most pious or the most educated or the most heroic people. He intentionally called together a community of misfits. Fishermen weren't known to be particularly holy, and certainly weren't well-educated. And the combination of Levi, the former tax collector, and Simon, the former zealot, was even potentially deadly. Tax collectors were considered tools of the empire, exploiting their own people for profit. But zealots were more than willing to use violence to accomplish what they believed was God's will, which is why they would often target tax collectors for assassination. Jesus's gospel of the kin(g)dom called each of the disciples to repentance and to a new way of life. They left behind their previous prejudices and philosophies, their previous ideas of what a successful life looked like, and took up the call to become like Jesus. This calling entailed becoming part of a new kind of family, spiritual siblings with some people they would have previously despised.

Even the apostle Paul, who had a prestigious religious pedigree, didn't believe he was chosen because he deserved to be a follower of Christ. To the contrary, Paul considered himself the least likely to be chosen because of how violently he persecuted the church. He called himself the "least of all God's people" (Ephesians 3:8) and "unworthy to be called an apostle" (1 Corinthians 15:9). But Paul understood how God's choosing works. God chose the Hebrew people from among all the ethnic groups of the world, not because they were the best, strongest, most numerous, or most righteous. No, God explicitly tells them they were chosen despite being the fewest and stiff-necked (cf. Deut. 7:7, 9:6). This is God's *modus operandi*; God chooses the disinherited, the overlooked, and the underestimated. God chooses the powerless to humiliate the powers. God chooses the ungodly to demonstrate God's righteousness. That's why I prefer to translate 1 Corinthians 1:26–31 this way:

> Brothers and sisters, think of what you were when you were called. Not many of you were wise by human standards; not many were influential; not many were of noble birth. But God chose the foolish ones of the world to shame the wise; God chose the weak ones of the world to shame the strong. God chose the lowly ones of this world and the despised ones—and the ones who are nobodies—to shut the mouths of the ones who think they're somebodies, so that no one may boast before him. It is because of him that you are in Christ Jesus, who has become for us wisdom from God—that is, our righteousness, holiness and redemption. Therefore, as it is written: "Let the one who boasts boast in the Lord."[1]

While the body of Christ may be made up of lowly and despised "nobodies" in the eyes of the world, God's choosing has made us holy and righteous "somebodies." The calling and choosing of God ennobles us and joins us to others in a diverse spiritual family.

DIVERSITY ON THE JOURNEY

I'm sure I don't have to tell you that religious communities aren't always spaces that honor the dignity of all people. We've seen how too often religious faith is used as a weapon, not a refuge. We already know that religious faith is often used to insulate the wealthy, privileged, and powerful from discomfort, criticism, or accountability. Far too often, religious faith divides people more than it unites. Religious faith can be structured in such a way that there are clear insiders and outsiders. And it's not always about beliefs or even practices. Sometimes it's even more superficial than that.

When I was a pastor in LA a few blocks from Skid Row, a new church began meeting on Sunday mornings in a nightclub space down the street from the theater where our church met. One Sunday, I was walking down the street as their service let out, and I couldn't believe what I was seeing. Every person who walked out the door looked like they'd just walked off the set of a music video or a photo shoot. I started calling it "Supermodel Church." My first thought was, "How could anyone who doesn't look or dress like a supermodel feel welcome there? How could someone who just spent the night in a tent on Skid Row walk into that worship gathering and feel like they belong?"

To be a community that's a refuge for misfits, to be that hospitable and affirming of all people, takes intentionality. It doesn't happen by accident. It starts with the conviction that diversity builds strength. It's vital that we can be our full selves—everything God has made us—and still be loved and belong in the family of

God. We must be crystal clear that what unites us isn't a list of doctrines we affirm, or how good we look when we dress up in our Sunday best—it also isn't our ethnic heritages or our taste in music. What unites us is our allegiance to Jesus, the Truly Human One, King of Kings, Prince of Peace. As Brené Brown has written, "True belonging doesn't require us to change who we are; it requires us to be who we are."[2]

Radical hospitality requires a framework flexible enough to allow people to be themselves. While most of the Christian world isn't well-known for this, there is a tradition that has made this a core value. Moravian Christians have popularized the saying, *"In essentials, unity; in non-essentials, liberty; in all things, love."* Moravians don't place things like the Bible, creeds, or sacred practices like communion and baptism in the "essentials" category. Instead, they consider these "ministerials," since they minister to us by pointing us to that which is essential. For Moravians, what's essential is six-fold: God creates (and creation is good); God redeems; God sustains (or blesses). In response, we have faith, love, and hope.[3] These six are less doctrines one must affirm and more of an awareness of our relational connection with the divine. Contextual aspects of our faith and cultural expressions like the music we sing, or the way we worship, or the language we speak, are called "incidentals." By relegating these cultural and contextual aspects of faith to a category even less essential than ministerials, Moravians undermine the project of White supremacy that has superimposed Western culture onto Christianity and exported them as a package. In contrast, Moravians believe diversity is a necessary part of the journey of faith.

At Roots we call our neighborhood gatherings "journey groups." We recognize that faith isn't a destination, it's a journey. So if we want Roots to be a refuge for misfits and a place of healing, we must give everyone space to learn and grow at their own pace. Just as in a healthy family children aren't expected to have adult responsibilities, a healthy spiritual community makes space for developmentally appropriate growth. But, likewise, a healthy family makes space for emerging adults to negotiate their independence and exercise appropriate leadership in a safe environment. Journey groups are spaces where family is forged with intentionality. We can proudly wear the "misfit" label because we know we belong in this community; our place in the family is secure.

THE (UN)PARABLE ABOUT A KIN(G)DOM PARTY

To help his hearers understand how God's family works, Jesus told many parables about the kin(g)dom. He compared the kin(g)dom to a wide range of odd things, from a valuable pearl to a buried treasure, even a fishing net (cf. Matthew 13). But there may only be one parable in which Jesus intends his followers to literally apply the story in their lives: the (un)parable of the dinner party.

As Luke tells it, Jesus was sharing a meal with Jewish religious leaders who were already suspicious of him. During this meal, Jesus noticed how those in attendance jockeyed for the best seats at the table, seats reserved for honored guests. So he gave them some free advice. Don't exalt yourself in the presence of your dinner host, Jesus said, or you may be humbled. Instead, humble yourself, so that you may be given special honor. I can imagine the people who'd quickly secured the seats of honor squirming a bit as Jesus glanced in their direction.

Then Jesus told his watchful hosts not to invite people for a party who could repay them for the honor. This must have struck his hosts as a bit odd, since they likely knew Jesus wasn't going to return the favor by inviting them to his own version of an interrogation dinner. He told them that instead of inviting people who could repay them, "when you give a banquet, invite the poor, the crippled, the lame, the blind, and you will be blessed. Although they cannot repay you, you will be repaid at the resurrection of the righteous" (Luke 14:13–14). Luke says one of the guests at the meal that night saw this as the right time to show their piety by toasting to those who would most assuredly be God's honored guests: themselves. That's what prompts Jesus to tell a parable:

> *Jesus replied: "A certain man was preparing a great banquet and invited many guests. At the time of the banquet he sent his servant to tell those who had been invited, 'Come, for everything is now ready.'*
>
> *"But they all alike began to make excuses. The first said, 'I have just bought a field, and I must go and see it. Please excuse me.'*
>
> *"Another said, 'I have just bought five yoke of oxen, and I'm on my way to try them out. Please excuse me.'*
>
> *"Still another said, 'I just got married, so I can't come.'*
>
> *"The servant came back and reported this to his master. Then the owner of the house became angry and ordered his servant,*

'Go out quickly into the streets and alleys of the town and bring in the poor, the crippled, the blind and the lame.'

"'Sir,' the servant said, 'what you ordered has been done, but there is still room.'

"Then the master told his servant, 'Go out to the roads and country lanes and compel them to come in, so that my house will be full. I tell you, not one of those who were invited will get a taste of my banquet.'" (Luke 14:16–24^{NIV})

While the kin(g)dom of God does not literally look like a valuable pearl, a buried treasure, or a fishing net, the kin(g)dom of God does actually look like a dinner party to which those on the margins have been invited. On the night when Jesus was betrayed, he gathered his closest disciples together for a meal. Around that table sat the misfits he'd called to follow him and who had become family. When Jesus describes the excuses some made for not coming to the party in his parable, they sound remarkably similar to real excuses people made when Jesus invited them to follow him as his disciple (Luke 9:57–62). Jesus, then, is the servant who reports to the master, "there is still room [in the house]."

Forging family in the way of Jesus literally requires making space at our tables for those who have been left out, cast aside, and pushed around. It often literally requires hosting a dinner and inviting people over. The kin(g)dom of God is a family in which there is literally always room for more. And the kin(g)dom of God is a family that publicly loves those who have been publicly maligned.

11 | LOVE IN PUBLIC

The Spirit of the Lord is on me,
because he has anointed me
to proclaim good news to the poor.
He has sent me to proclaim freedom for the prisoners
and recovery of sight for the blind,
to set the oppressed free,
to proclaim the year of the Lord's favor.

Luke 4:18–19[NIV]

THE MURDER OF GEORGE FLOYD

All I could do was lay in bed scrolling through videos on my phone, thinking that would help me fall asleep. It was May 26, 2020, at close to 4:00 A.M.. What I saw next would mark an inflection point in my life. In fact, the video I viewed early that morning would change the world. It was a video of a police officer brutally restraining a man while he and nearby onlookers begged him to show mercy. The man being held down pleaded desperately for the officer to let up, crying out for his mother, and saying, "I can't breathe." But that officer knelt on his neck with such cavalier disdain, hands in his pocket, smirk on his face that his body language said, "Your life doesn't matter." As I watched I grew increasingly confused and anxious. "Were they really going to just kill this man?" I thought. "Was this cop really going to murder this man in cold blood in broad daylight?"

Minutes went by—over nine minutes. Then the man just lay there, lifeless. "What did I just see? How could this happen?" I thought as I checked the timestamp. I looked for the location. *Minneapolis!? Hours ago!?* There was no going back to sleep. I was awake now.

And for the next several weeks, months, over a year, we lived at the epicenter of a world-wide resurgence of a resistance movement to racism and police brutality. I thought of myself as deeply committed to racial justice and had been trying to lead followers of Jesus to resist racism and embody the reconciling power of God for decades. Yet, by this point, I'd fallen under the persuasive influence of those who teach that followers of Jesus should stay out of politics. I'd been taught that to be a peacemaker meant to be neutral, to not take sides, and I'd believed that.

DUPED BY BOTHSIDESING

While I was still in seminary, I started to become a bothsideser. If you're not familiar with "bothsidesing," it's when a false equivalence is made either to claim that "both sides" of a contentious matter are equally good or equally bad. An example from journalism is when reporters are tempted to give equal time to opposing views on climate change. On one side is the decades-old, overwhelming consensus of climate scientists that global warming is the result of human pollution and an existential threat to human life. On the other side are fringe voices of denial that represent an extreme outlier viewpoint. "By giving credence to the other side, the media gives an impression of being fair to its subject, but in doing so often provides credibility to an idea that most might view as unmerited."[1] To give the impression that both sides are equally valid when they aren't often produces paralyzing confusion, dissuades action, and therefore serves to prevent real solutions to dire problems.

My bothsidesing began with a rejection of the Religious Right's warmongering, disgust at their moral hypocrisy, and an increasing embrace of Christian nonviolence. At the time, I believed that faithfulness to Jesus and his kin(g)dom also required rejection of politics, because the nonviolence of Jesus was incompatible with the violence inherent in the political process. This helped me distance myself from the self-righteousness of White Evangelical conservatives who very nearly equated the Republican Party with Christianity itself. But the White American Evangelical world is so entrenched in two-party partisan politics that refusing to identify as a Republican or conservative often leads to being labeled a liberal or progressive—a grave condemnation. To avoid this sort of accusation, I learned from many of the White voices I was listening to at that time to remain neutral and objective in order to appear above the fray of politics. More than a few times I repeated the now cliché line: "I'm too conservative for liberals and too liberal for conservatives." I even compared this supposed neutrality with Jesus's own ministry by citing Jesus's refusal to decide between two brothers on their inheritance (Luke 12:14). And I wrongfully attributed neutrality to Jesus when he said, "give back to Caesar what is Caesar's, and to God what is God's" (Matthew 22:21). I even used the inclusion of both a zealot and a tax collector among Jesus's disciples as evidence that bipartisanship was a kingdom value. Looking back, I'm embarrassed that I was so naive and ashamed that I was so easily deceived.

Bothsidesing is really only conceivable when the stakes are extremely low. When the sides in question represent a dangerous threat, or dehumanizing oppression, bothsidesing becomes inexcusable. In fact, bothsidesing can only be sustained long-term from a place of substantial privilege, insulated from any real harm that could be caused by bad politics. That's why my bothsidesing unraveled when Donald Trump ran for president in 2015. His blatant racism, misogyny, and xenophobia destroyed all my attempts to remain neutral, which I never really was, because my inaction was default support for the status quo. After 2015, I could no longer in good conscience stand idly by and watch people whom I love, and the neighbors Jesus calls me to love, be dehumanized and discriminated against. I could no longer pretend that matters of justice were mere differences of opinion.

The Jesus to whom I've devoted my life reveals a God who is the liberator of the oppressed Hebrews from slavery in Egypt, making the Exodus the very paradigm of salvation throughout scripture. Jesus reveals the God who sees, protects, and makes promises to Hagar, an exploited Egyptian female slave. We would do well to remember that she is the very first person in scripture to name God (Genesis 16:13)! Jesus reveals the God who is spoken of in Mary's "Magnificat" as having "pulled down the powerful from their thrones and lifted up the lowly," "filled the hungry with good things and sent the rich away empty-handed" (Luke 1:46–55). It was Jesus who taught that neglecting the weightier matter of justice for the appearance of purity makes one a hypocrite (cf. Matthew 23:23). And it was Jesus who said, "The Spirit of the Lord is upon me, because the Lord has anointed me. He has sent me to preach good news to the poor, to proclaim release to the prisoners, and recovery of sight to the blind, to liberate the oppressed, and to proclaim the year of the Lord's favor" (Luke 4:18–19CEB).

Of course a God who sides with the oppressed is offensive to those with social privilege and power. They will inevitably ask, "Doesn't God love everyone—even the rich and powerful?" Of course God does! God's kin(g)dom liberates everyone! But liberation comes to the powerful in a very different way than it comes to the dispossessed. As Mennonite pastor, Jonny Rashid, writes in *Jesus Takes a Side*, "Everyone is invited to the table; however for the powerful among us, the invitation comes with a cost. For everyone, the invitation is to liberation, which the oppressed already welcome. The oppressors, however, must risk surrendering everything to take Jesus's side"[2]. Those whom Jesus calls to be his disciples are offered a choice: Will we embrace Jesus's kin(g)dom movement and the liberation it entails, or will we reject him? Wealth and comfort can be so seductive. Many will see themselves in the "rich young ruler" who went away sad because they too found the cost of discipleship far too great (cf. Mark 10:17–22).

But for those who accept the call and take a seat at the table of liberation, a transformation of our loves begins.

THE TRANSITIVE PROPERTY OF LOVE

I may not be very good at math, but I do know that in math there's a principle called the transitive property. An example would be: If $A = B$ and $B = C$, then $A = C$. In loving relationships, there's a similar kind of transitive property. When you deeply love someone—over time perhaps, but inevitably—you begin to love what they love. That doesn't mean that people in loving relationships will always agree on everything or have the same taste. In fact, the two in the relationship might be complete opposites and have drastically different taste. After all, "opposites attract," right? But, even if two people in a loving relationship are polar opposites, over time, each person in the relationship will at the very least develop an appreciation for what the other loves because of how much they love the other person. They will begin to see with the eyes of the one they love.

Osheta and I have been married for over two decades, and I can tell you that we are about as different as two people can be. But, of course, I love her deeply, so at the very least I can appreciate the things she loves. For example, Osheta loves romantic comedies, and I typically can't stand them. But, over the years, I've watched a bunch of them with her because I love her, and not all of them were terrible.

One of her favorites is *The Holiday*, starring Cameron Diaz, Jude Law, Kate Winslet, and Jack Black. Diaz's character

lives in LA, and Winslet's character lives in the English coun-
tryside, and they swap houses for a much-needed vacation. In
the process, Diaz's character falls in love with Winslet's character's brother who lives in England, played by Jude Law. Meanwhile, back in LA, Winslet's character is trying to get over a
toxic ex-boyfriend. In the process, she befriends a gentlemanly
older man named Arthur who lives nearby. She soon learns that
he has a prestigious pedigree in Old Hollywood as a retired
movie maker. He shares with her the beauty of old films with
an emphasis on leading ladies. As she grows closer and closer
with Arthur, she develops a love for the movies he made. As she
helps him gain the confidence to take the stage and accept a lifetime achievement award, she gains the confidence to maintain
healthy boundaries with her ex. The more she cares for Arthur,
the more she begins to care about what Arthur cares about. And
Arthur's love for old movies becomes Winslet's character's love
for them as well.

When we love someone, we want to share with them the things
that we love deeply. We want them to share in our experience of
joy, excitement, and fulfillment. Think about anything that you've
put your heart and soul into, anything that is so meaningful to
you that it takes up a significant part of your life. Naturally, you
want those whom you love to love those things too.

This is what it's like to be loved by God and then have God's
love transform our loves. The more we grow in love, the more
we will naturally come to love what God loves. And as it turns
out, God loves people and *shalom*-justice. God loves *shalom*-justice
because it's when people are whole, flourishing in their bearing

of God's image, thriving in relationship with others and with the creation. In fact, God loves the world in such a way that God sent God's unique Son into the world not to condemn the world, but so that the world might be saved through him (cf. John 3:16). God loves when human beings love one another and make their world a habitat of love. To love our neighbors well, we must care about the policies and politics that affect all our lives.

One of the biggest mistakes I've made when it comes to following Jesus was thinking I could opt out of politics. I used to think that because Jesus's kin(g)dom is not like any other kingdom in this world, that this meant I shouldn't participate in worldly things like voting, I shouldn't want to learn about the platforms and positions of various political candidates and shouldn't advocate for any particular policies. But what I later realized is that it's a lot easier for me to opt out of politics, with little or no negative effects, than it is for my neighbors or even members of my own family. Regardless of who the mayor is, who the police chief is, who the governor is, who my congresspersons are, or even who the president is, my life will pretty much remain the same. I'm ashamed to say I realized far too slowly that this wasn't the case for a lot of people for whom I deeply care. Even if my life wasn't dramatically affected by the policies being enacted, many millions of other people's lives were being severely impacted every day. I realized that my privilege had obscured my perspective on the very real consequences politics have on people who haven't been afforded the same social advantages I have.

I'm not a woman, so I'm not impacted by policies and laws that restrict affordable and accessible family planning resources and health care.

I'm not an immigrant, so I'm not impacted by policies and laws that restrict visas, revoke protective status for people who have lived here their whole lives, or cut off travel from entire countries.

I'm not a member of the LGBTQ+ community, so I'm not impacted by policies and laws that target queer folks or restrict their access to their human rights.

I'm not a follower of a religion like Islam that is misunderstood and feared, so I'm not impacted by policies and laws that discriminate against Muslims (or members of other religions for that matter).

I'm not a person living with disability, so I'm not impacted by policies and laws that prevent disabled persons from having full access to the same things as abled-bodied people.

In each of these ways and probably more, by virtue of my identity relative to others in society, I've been afforded unjust advantages. The politics of Jesus teach me not to luxuriate in that privilege but to leverage it to demand justice for those who lack it. The politics of Jesus teach me to settle down, plant roots, and seek the *shalom* of the city to which I've been called. The politics of Jesus call me to see those who are marginalized by the powers that be and to seek the common good of all who are feared, hated, marginalized, excluded, afflicted, and oppressed. The politics of Jesus teach me how to be part of a different kind of family—one that is not constituted by genetics, but by our common allegiance to Jesus—a family for the sake of others.

HMONG AMERICANS FOR BLACK LIVES

Another one of the officers who was on the scene that day while Derek Chauvin was murdering George Floyd in broad daylight was Tou Thao, who is Hmong American. Instead of defending Floyd's human rights and protecting him from being killed, Thao used his authority to manage the crowd of bystanders who were demanding Floyd's release from Chauvin's deadly grip. He positioned his body between Chauvin's and the crowd and called for them to remain calm. That is why he was charged with aiding and abetting murder and manslaughter.

In the wake of George Floyd's murder, the Twin Cities exploded with activism and calls for the arrests of all four officers on the scene. As difficult as it may be now to imagine, it took four days for Derek Chauvin to be arrested for his role in Floyd's death and nine days for the other officers at the scene to be charged as accessories. During those intervening days, Osheta and I participated in many prayer gatherings, marches, and protests. We gathered together with our church to pray, we gathered together with other ministers and clergy to march, and we gathered with our neighbors in Minneapolis to protest and demand justice.

Meanwhile, our church had asked Der Lor, who is Hmong American, to join our pastoral team as he discerned his next call in ministry. Over the course of the previous year, he and his family had become cherished members of our misfit community, and we were thrilled to call him to serve alongside us as a pastor. But at the same time that the Twin Cities was experiencing a well-deserved uprising, tensions were also rising between the Black and Hmong communities. Tou Thao's presence at Floyd's murder became a flash point of online vitriol that threatened to spill over into the streets. This prompted pastor Der to take action. He and I headed down to the 3rd Precinct where thousands of protesters had gathered to demand justice. Groups were there that day marching, groups handing out water and other supplies, and throngs of people holding signs, kneeling, and shouting "Justice for George Floyd!" Officers were stationed on the roof of the precinct armed with rifles trained at the crowd. But in stark contrast to some of the coverage that portrayed protests in Minneapolis as violent, what we witnessed that day was closer to an open-air church service than a riot. Thousands knelt in a moment of silence as Black community leaders led us, sometimes urging those gathered to keep the streets clean by picking up trash we see on the ground. Der and I spent hours there that afternoon, participating in the calls, the silences, and talking with others gathered there. Pastor Der held his sign in the air, which simply read, "Hmong Americans for Black Lives."

That simple act of solidarity was nevertheless a profound expression of the deep spiritual formation Der has experienced as a disciple of Jesus. Rather than allowing the din of division between the Black and Hmong communities to sideline him, he stepped out in faith and hope to demonstrate God's love. It's moments like these that forged family in the way of Jesus. It's courage like his that is a prophetic witness to the powers that seek to divide us.

PROPHETIC WITNESS

One of the aspects of loving our neighbors well that many followers of Jesus in the United States seem to struggle with is protest. I've heard over and over that protest doesn't seem very Christ-like because it makes demands upon the government, and demanding justice from the government can make White American Christians very uneasy. There was even a time when I doubted that protest could be faithfully employed by followers of Jesus because of my indoctrination through bothsidesing. But thankfully the prophetic witness of the Black Church in America has been an ever-present teacher that has disabused me of theologies that depend upon apathy and complacency. The Black Church in America has taught me that in order to love our neighbors well, as Jesus commands, we *must* care about the politics that divide and oppress us all. As Dr. Cornel West has famously said, "Justice is what love looks like in public."[3]

In fact, this is precisely what we see when we read about Jesus's ministry throughout the Gospels. If we survey Matthew, Mark, and Luke passage by passage with eyes trained on "love in public," what we find there might surprise us. Each Gospel spends a significant portion of its text telling stories about Jesus demonstrating love in public. Here are some of the things the Gospels show us Jesus doing: (1) feeding the hungry (the poor); (2) including someone who had been formally excluded from the community; (3) healing the afflicted (who were often also excluded); (4) liberating the spiritually oppressed; and (5) recognizing the faith of an unlikely or overlooked person. Even if we leave out passages where Jesus teaches people to do the things he was doing—which he does a lot, especially in parables—these love in public stories alone constitute 16 percent of Matthew, 20 percent of Luke, and 26 percent of Mark. Justice—demonstrating love in public—was Jesus's politics. This was how Jesus demonstrated the kin(g)dom of God. For Jesus, the kin(g)dom of God looks like enough food for everyone; enough loving community for everyone; wholeness and physical well-being for everyone; freedom from oppression for everyone; recognition of gifts and callings of everyone.

Jesus had no compunction about calling to account those who abused their power over the vulnerable. Jesus did this at a pivotal moment in his ministry: the very first Holy Week. On that first Holy Week, Jesus entered Jerusalem and overturned the tables of the money changers in the temple courts in a public act of protest.

> *On reaching Jerusalem, Jesus entered the temple courts and began driving out those who were buying and selling there. He overturned the tables of the money changers and the benches of those selling doves, and would not allow anyone to carry merchandise through the temple courts. And as he taught them, he said, "Is it not written: 'My house will be called a house of prayer for all nations'? But you have made it 'a den of robbers.'"*
>
> *The chief priests and the teachers of the law heard this and began looking for a way to kill him, for they feared him, because the whole crowd was amazed at his teaching.* (Mark 11:15–18[NIV])

Contrary to popular opinion, this was no spontaneous act of rage. Jesus deliberately staged this public protest, and his declarations were precise echoes of prophetic speech directed at corrupt leaders and their systems of oppression. Jesus was walking in the prophetic footsteps of the Hebrew prophets who had gone before him. In particular, Jesus was calling to mind the prophet Jeremiah, who centuries earlier had delivered a prophetic word to Jerusalem about justice and the temple.

The word that came to Jeremiah from the Lord: "Stand in the gate of the Lord's house, and proclaim there this word, and say, Hear the word of the Lord, all you men of Judah who enter these gates to worship the Lord. Thus says the Lord of hosts, the God of Israel: Amend your ways and your deeds, and I will let you dwell in this place. Do not trust in these deceptive words: 'This is the temple of the Lord, the temple of the Lord, the temple of the Lord.'

"For if you truly amend your ways and your deeds, if you truly execute justice one with another, if you do not oppress the sojourner, the fatherless, or the widow, or shed innocent blood in this place, and if you do not go after other gods to your own harm, then I will let you dwell in this place, in the land that I gave of old to your fathers forever." (Jeremiah 7:1–7)

Jeremiah called out Judah for their hypocrisy. They thought they could stand idly by while the vulnerable in society were unjustly treated as long as they had the temple. Religious worship papered over their neglect of the poor, and they thought they could love God without loving those made in God's image. They'd even created a jingle of sorts: "This is the temple of the Lord, the temple of the Lord, the temple of the Lord." But God spoke through the prophet saying in effect, "This building is not what keeps you in covenant with me—it's your faithfulness to my way of love! And if you think I haven't noticed your indifference to injustice, you're very wrong!"

Not only does Jesus indict the temple leaders for the greed and corruption of the money-lenders, Jesus also connects this call for justice toward the vulnerable with a prophecy from Isaiah about God creating a new covenant with people from all the ethnic groups of the world—even including people excluded due to their gender and sexuality.

> *This is what the Lord says: "Maintain justice and do what is right, for my salvation is close at hand and my righteousness will soon be revealed. Blessed is the one who does this—the person who holds it fast, who keeps the Sabbath without desecrating it, and keeps their hands from doing any evil."*
>
> *Let no foreigner who is bound to the Lord say, "The Lord will surely exclude me from his people." And let no eunuch complain, "I am only a dry tree."*
>
> *For this is what the Lord says: "To the eunuchs who keep my Sabbaths, who choose what pleases me and hold fast to my covenant—to them I will give within my temple and its walls a memorial and a name better than sons and daughters; I will give them an everlasting name that will endure forever. And foreigners who bind themselves to the Lord to minister to him, to love the name of the Lord, and to be his servants, all who keep the Sabbath without desecrating it and who hold fast to my covenant—these I will bring to my holy mountain and give them joy in my house of prayer. Their burnt offerings and sacrifices will be accepted on my altar; for my house will be called a house of prayer for all nations."* (Isaiah 56:1–7[NIV])

Jesus's public protest in the temple courts marks a climactic moment in his ministry—one that sets him on a collision course with the powers that be. And this protest is both a condemnation of the religious establishment and a reminder of God's dream for a new covenant community made up of those who had formerly been excluded. Including foreigners and eunuchs into God's covenant people would be God's witness to the world that God loves everyone and God is restoring *shalom.*

Following Jesus into a new kind of family means joining together with others to become holy disrupters of the status quo. It means taking action when we see neglect or abuse in our cities. It means standing in solidarity with vulnerable communities and rejecting the forces of division. It means siding with those oppressed and rejecting false equivalencies. It means loving our neighbors enough to demand justice and equity from elected officials. It means organizing and mobilizing in our neighborhoods and cities to make sure no one is left out or cast aside. It means publicly embodying the love of God as a prophetic witness.

ACKNOWLEDGMENTS

This book is a dream come true—a dream that began a decade ago when I was in a theology class taught by Michelle Clifton. While teaching on baptism, she said, "water is thicker than blood." At that very moment, I knew I needed to write my story of forged family in Christ. Since then, I began dreaming I'd one day have the opportunity to write this very book, and here it is! Thank you, Michelle.

There's no way I could thank everyone who's contributed to my story. That would take an entire second book. So this is merely a nowhere-near-complete list. And, by thanking someone here, I'm in no way making them share culpability for the ideas in this book. So please don't blame them for any of my mistakes or "heresies." If they are thanked here, it is because they made the writing of this book possible, or they're part of my forged family, or they've pointed me toward Jesus in some significant way. You're reading this book because of them.

I'll start by thanking Naomi Thorson Krueger for connecting me with Lisa Kloskin. Thank you for believing I have a story worth telling and for your insights into publishing world. Since

I've known you, you've been a fierce advocate for me and my family and I'm so grateful. Thank you, Lisa, for accepting my book proposal and walking alongside me as I wrestled with insecurities and made several changes to the book's structure. You were patient and wise, a steady hand throughout the process. And thanks to the whole team at Broadleaf Books for giving me the chance to write this book. I don't think it could have found a better home.

URBANA

The seeds that would grow to become this book were planted in Urbana, Illinois, where I came to faith as a teenager, but not before I was welcomed and loved as a child by ministers at the Urbana Vineyard. Thank you, Hank Sanford, for your faithful presence and joy. How could I ever forget the youth group worship gatherings you led in "God's Garage"? Thank you, Ben Hoerr, for your pastoral care and for remembering me all those years later when we saw each other again at a conference. Thank you, Chris Sandel, for opening your home to me and teaching me "the meaning of life" (I still have the tattoo!).

Thank you, Gary "Papa G" Grogan, for speaking what the Spirit told you to all those years ago and for baptizing me. I have no doubt your obedience that night saved my life. Thank you to all the many "aunties" and "uncles" at Urbana Assembly of God (now Stone Creek Church) who became my family when I was still 16. To Terry Hutson, for your generous gifts and heartfelt encouragement; to Rob King, for giving me opportunities to lead youth; to Bonnie Grogan, for your hospitality; to Rob Siedenburg, for opening the scriptures to me and praying with such passion; to Rick Breitenfeldt, for giving me my first desk job; and to Dale and Betsy Innes, Dave Rees, Eddie De La Rosa, and so many more, thank you! You will always be my home church.

Thank you to the spiritual siblings from Urbana who are part of my forged family: Nathan Rinehart, my day one who invited me to your baptism. Rob Gardner, I'll never forget our days as interns together. Felix Bunn, you always made me feel like family. Thank you to Carrie Innes, Tyler Bergfield, Ruth and Rebecca Matthew, Ian Cler, Noah Harris, Noah Schroeder, Jason Jackson, Jeff Masters, Jordan Bradford, Eric Forsyth, Wesley Cheong, Lynette "Freddie" Karulkar, Bernie Ranchero, and so many more. Thank you to everyone who ever prayed for me at Excel or Sudden Impact.

Most of all, thank you, Uncle Terry Austria, for mentoring me, opening your life to me, teaching me how to read the scriptures, teaching me to how to pray, and giving me opportunities to lead and serve. This book is because of you.

NEW ORLEANS

My story took a profound turn when I sensed the call to move to New Orleans to attend Bible college. Thank you to all those who walked with me through those years before and after hurricane Katrina. Thank you, Jimi for being a theological comrade (we'll always be the "demons in the dorms") and Melissa Orekoya: thank you for opening your home to me, Osheta, and Tyson when we didn't know where we to go. Thank you to Corey Hicks (and Ma Hicks!) for making me part of your family. Thank you to my roommates, Ryan Galashan (my Canadian brother), and Guillermo Nava (my Mexican brother). Thank you, Orion Russ, for being the protective brother I never had. And thank you, Jason Brunet, for teaching me about the harmfulness of toxic masculinity. Thank you to my philosophy discussion buddies, Myron Crockett and Matt DeGier. You challenged me to think in new ways.

Thank you to my professors from Bible college: Richard Miller, for teaching me hermeneutics, partnering with me in web design, and showing me how to be a free thinker. Thank you, Joan Millar, for your boldness and your faith. You inspired me. And, thank you, Teresa Johnson Reiger. You taught me so much, challenged me, and exposed me to ways of thinking about God that set me on a theological pilgrimage I'm still on.

Thank you, Kevin and Sandy Brown, for being role models for Osheta and me when we were newlyweds. Thank you, Kevin, for giving me my first job after graduation, teaching me about incarnational ministry, and introducing me to Christian Community Development. I'll never forget the two years I served with you in Hollygrove at Trinity Christian Community. They were so formative. Thank you, Evelyn Turner and Earl Williams. You two taught me so much just by being around you. Thank you for your faithful witness.

Shout out to the youth I served at Canal Street Assembly of God (now House of Prayer AG) and Boutte Assembly of God (now Life Church AG).

Thank you, Mike and Christina Hogg, for welcoming me and my family to Canal Street Presbyterian church and treating us like family. I'll never forget how all you taught me about pastoral ministry and the way you shepherded us through the storm. Shout out to all my siblings in Christ from Canal Pres.

Thank you to Missy and Mickey Lane for being Osheta's godparents, our children's forged grandparents, and for taking us in after the storm.

CAMBRIDGE AND BOSTON

When Katrina uprooted us and we landed in Boston, I never imagined it would grow to feel like home, and we'd forge so much family there. Thank you, Dan and Kathy Szatkowski, for being our pastors through some of the most challenging years of our lives. You were gracious, kind, and encouraging. Thank you, Glenn and Dianne Knowles. I often think about a conversation when you encouraged me to not wait around until I get a PhD to write a book. Thank you! And thank you, Tracy Wemett, Bill Boxx, Dakota Pippins, Marcos and Nika Elugardo, Nathan Abramson and Sara Ontiveros, Paul and Jan Bothwell, Chuck and Laura Van Hise, and everyone at Cambridgeport Baptist Church for being our spiritual siblings.

Thank you so much, Larry Kim. You're such an important part of my forged family. I couldn't imagine writing this book without your input. Thank you for reading early drafts of chapters and for all the many years of support and encouragement.

Thank you, Albert and Emily Chen (the best church planting partners!), Grace Lee, Benny Diep, Leslie Moore, Henry Johnson, and everyone at Cambridge Community Fellowship Church (now Central Square Church).

Thank you, Dave Capozzi, for dragging me to a Switchfoot concert and for helping me make it through seminary! And to the whole Tanks to Tractors crew: Tim Colegrove, Matt Modaff, Erik Nordbye, and everyone else who cycled through. Thank you to Omar and J. J. Reyes, Christina Tinglof, Brian Estrella, Andrew Mook, Rashad Clemons, Annery Miranda, Eugene Schneeberg, Fred and Terri Elliot-Hart, Emmanuel Tikili, Vince Bantu, and Ben Rey.

To Ricky Grant and Mako Nagasawa, thank you for allowing me to serve with you on the teaching team at Rescued Church. Serving alongside you two is one of my fondest memories from Boston.

I owe a huge thank you to Matt Gibson, who has been a mentor and friend since my earliest days in seminary. You have probably called me and checked in on me weekly for over a decade. And I've heard God's voice through you more times than I can count. Thank you!

Thank you to all my amazing professors at Gordon-Conwell (CUME). Thank you, Soong-Chan Rah, for introducing me to postcolonial theology and the ECC, which opened so many doors. Thank you, Eldin Villafañe, for introducing me to Heschel and liberation theology. Thank you to Doug and Judy Hall and Jeff Bass for introducing me to systems thinking in the context of urban ministry. That has been invaluable!

Thank you to the whole crew over at the Emmanuel Gospel Center (EGC). Thank you, Brian Corcoran, Steve Daman, Ruth Wong, Jin Min Lee, and everyone else!

While I was in Boston, I forged a lot of family around the country through church planting connections and theology circles. I need to thank a bunch of people for their influence on my story. Thank you, Thomas Jay Oord for all the academic and publishing opportunities you've given me! Thank you, Rodney Thomas Jr. and Joshua Tom for being the best theology moderators on the web! Thank you to Kurt Willems, Pierre Keys, and Dwayne Polk for being my partners in theological exploration. Thank you to Drew Hart for being my AAR roommate.

Thank you to my ECC family: José Humphreys, Michael Carrion (the Bishop of the Bronx!), Efrain "Brother E" Alicea (I miss you, bro!), Dan and Rebecca Stringer, Marco Ambriz, Kirk Davis, Joel Sommer, Alex Gee, Lisa Sharon Harper, Drew Jackson, and Shaun Marshall. Thank you, Dominique Gilliard, for giving me the opportunity to facilitate a racial righteousness cohort. Thank you, Howard Burgoyne, Jason Condon, Steve Cushing, Rob Fairbanks, and Efrem Smith.

I also need to give a huge thank you to Dennis Edwards. You have been such a faithful and inspirational mentor to me. Thank you for all the ways you've encouraged me.

LOS ANGELES

Moving to Los Angeles was a huge shift in my journey of faith, not all for the good. In spite of the intense challenges, our time in LA forged some really important family. I have to give a huge thank you to Manny Chavarria. It feels like we were destined to be brothers. Our lives have mirrored one another's in some eerie and amazing ways. Thank you for being one of the earliest readers of draft chapters of this book. Your feedback was crucial. Thank you to my dear sister, Hannah Sims. Serving alongside you forged us into family and I'm so grateful. Thank you to Delonte Gholston, Naomi Abella, David and Amy Park, Kim Johnson, Eugene San Jose, John and Jude Tiersma Watson, James and Amy Townsend, Ryan and Nora Murray, Tim and Mariann Reardon, Gabe Veas, Joshua Trujillo, Tripp Fuller, and so many more! Thank you, Jason Brooks, for showing me the kin(g)dom of God through your Sunday night dinners. I'll never forget the amazing conversations we had about theology.

Thank you to Josh "J.W." Buck and Jer Swigart for being early readers of draft chapters. You both helped me rethink my approach to this book and I'm so grateful!

Thank you so much, Blake and Debbie Waltman. You are the definition of forged family! Thank you for adopting our family and being our children's godparents. Thank you for supporting us all these years and for making memories with us.

SAINT PAUL (TWIN CITIES)

Moving to the Twin Cities and serving the Roots community has been the best move for our family. We love it here and so many wonderful people have become family. Thank you to Dave and Terri Churchill for welcoming us to Saint Paul and helping us become Minnesotans. Thank you, Greg and Shelley Boyd, Kevin Callahan (thank you for encouraging me to use "Forged Family" in the title of the book!) Der and Alice Lor, Stephanie and J. D. O'Brien, Mike and Ann Hotz, Anne Vining, T. David Starks (the best officemate I've ever had), Emily Morrison, Edrin Williams, Luke Swanson, Micah Witham, and too many to name.

Thank you to all the precious misfits of Roots Moravian Church. It's an honor and a privilege to serve as one of your pastors. Thank you so much, Kirsten Morissette, Darin Mather, Emmanuel and Amy Speare, Zong Thao and Miranda Xiong, Mama Janie, Renee and Matty Spillum. (Thank you so much, Matty, for reading and giving feedback on early drafts of this book!) Tobin and Caroline Vollmar, Tim Krueger, Joel and Dominique Holwerda, Mike and April Schellman, Desta and Lydia Anulo, Ben and Rose Eisenreich, Kayla Estrada Roth and Rafa Estrada Moncada, Jon and Johanna Moseng, Amanda Johnson, Rachel Martin Asproth and Iñaki Martin Cossio, Amy Wells, Tiffani and Scott Glime, and many others.

Thank you to Roots alumni Seng Bum Michael Yoo and Cho Long Kim, Juice and Ginger Montezon, Anna and Andrew Hill, Pablo and MyLinh Sanchez, Matt and Patricia Nguyen, Ross Holmes and Camille Leigh Tinnin, Tou and Alisa Xiong, Katrina and Andrew Wu, and so many more!

Thank you to our new Moravian siblings in Christ: Betsy Miller, Bruce Nelson, Amy Gohdes-Luhman, Charlie McDonald, Sylvie Hauser, and so many others. We're excited to be a part of such a rich legacy.

Most of all, I want to thank my partner in life, my best friend, and my favorite person, Osheta Moore. We've grown up together and you've always believed in me. Thank you for making space for me to write this book. You have been by my side this whole time forging family every step of the way. There's no one else in the world I want to be on this adventure we call life with more than you! I love you!

To my kids, Tyson, T. J., and Trinity: I hope this book
gives you a glimpse into the broader family you're a
part of. And I pray that one day you'll know
their love the way I do.

NOTES

CHAPTER 1

1 Brooks, David. "The Nuclear Family Was a Mistake," *The Atlantic*, March 2020, https://www.theatlantic.com/magazine/archive/2020/03/the-nuclear-family-was-a-mistake/605536/

2 Brooks, "The Nuclear Family Was a Mistake."

3 Angelou, Maya, *Twitter*, November 28, 2021, https://twitter.com/DrMayaAngelou/status/1464980088877953024?s=20

4 Snodgrass, Klyne, *Who God Says You Are: A Christian Understanding of Identity* (Eerdmans, 2018), p. 88.

5 Jennings, Willie James, *The Christian Imagination: Theology and the Origins of Race* (Yale Press, 2010), p. 265.

6 Florer-Bixler, Melissa, *How to Have an Enemy: Righteous Anger & the Work of Peace* (Herald Press, 2021), p. 112.

7 Wright, N. T., *Justification: God's Plan & Paul's Vision* (IVP Academic, 2009), p. 23.

8 Willard, Dallas, *The Divine Conspiracy: Rediscovering Our Hidden Life in God* (HarperCollins, 1998), p. 42.

9 DeSilva, David, *Honor, Patronage, Kinship & Purity: Unlocking New Testament Culture* (IVP Academic, 2000), pp. 179–180, 193.

10 Rah, Soong-Chan, *The Next Evangelicalism: Freeing the Church from Western Cultural Captivity* (IVP, 2009), pp. 29–30.

11 Rah, Soong-Chan and Mark Charles, *Unsettling Truths: The Ongoing Dehumanizing Legacy of the Doctrine of Discovery* (IVP, 2019), p. 34.

NOTES

12 Emerson, Micheal O. and Christian Smith, *Divided by Faith: Evangelical Religion and the Problem of Race in America* (Oxford Press, 2000), p. 76.

13 Emerson and Smith, *Divided by Faith*, p. 90.

14 Twiss, Richard, *One Church, Many Tribes: Following Jesus the Way God Made You* (Regal Books, 2000), p. 175.

15 Isasi-Díaz, Ada María, "The Kin-dom of God: A *Mujerista* Proposal," in *In Our Own Voices: Latino/a Renditions of Theology* (Orbis Books, 2010), Benjamín Valentín, editor, p. 173.

16 Isasi-Díaz., "The Kin-dom of God," p. 186.

CHAPTER 2

1 Barringer, Laura and Scot McKnight, *A Church Called Tov: Forming a Goodness Culture That Resists Abuses of Power and Promotes Healing* (Tyndall, 2020).

2 Rohr, Richard, *Things Hidden: Scripture as Spirituality* (Franciscan Media, 2008), p. 25.

3. Cuss, Steve, *Managing Leadership Anxiety: Yours and Theirs* (Thomas Nelson, 2019).

4 "The Doxology" refers to a hymn that is commonly sung in several Christian traditions. Its lyrics are: "Praise God from whom all blessings flow. Praise him all creatures here below. Praise him above ye heavenly hosts. Praise Father, Son, and Holy Ghost. Amen." Some traditions have modified the lyrics to be gender neutral. [https://en.wikipedia.org/wiki/Doxology#%22Praise_God,_from_whom_all_blessings_flow%22]

CHAPTER 3

1 St. Augustine of Hippo, *On the Trinity*, Book IX.

2 Baker Fletcher, Karen. *Dancing with God: The Trinity from a Womanist Perspective* (Chalice, 2006), pp. 44–45.

3 Reeves, Michael, *Delighting in the Trinity: An Introduction to the Christian Faith* (IVP Academic, 2012), p. 103.

NOTES

CHAPTER 4

1 Singh, Maanvi, "How Do Refugee Teens Build Resilience?" *WFSU Public Media* (July 30, 2017), https://news.wfsu.org/2017-07-30/how-do-refugee-teens-build-resilience. Study referenced: "Resilience in Context: A Brief and Culturally Grounded Measure for Syrian Refugee and Jordanian Host-Community Adolescents," https://doi.org/10.1111/cdev.12868.

CHAPTER 5

1 Wright, N. T., *Matthew For Everyone, Part 2: Chapters 16–28* (Westminster John Knox Press, 2004), p. 35.

2 Wright, *Matthew For Everyone, Part 2*, p. 36.

3 Florer-Bixler, *How to Have an Enemy*, p. 75.

CHAPTER 6

1 Foster Wallace, David, *This Is Water: Some Thoughts, Delivered on a Significant Occasion, about Living a Compassionate Life* (Little, Brown and Company, 2009).

2 Credit to Larry Kim for being the first person I heard this from.

3 Rah, Soong-Chan, *Many Colors: Cultural Intelligence for a Changing Church* (Moody Publishers, 2010), p. 28.

4 Pearcey, Nancy R., Total Truth: Liberating Christianity from Its Cultural Captivity (Crossway Books, 2004), p. 47 as quoted in Rah, Soong-Chan, *Many Colors: Cultural Intelligence for a Changing Church* (Moody Publishers, 2010), p. 29.

5 NPR, "Read Martin Luther King Jr.'s 'I Have a Dream' speech in its entirety" (January 16, 2023) https://www.npr.org/2010/01/18/122701268/i-have-a-dream-speech-in-its-entirety.

6 Twiss, Richard, *One Church, Many Tribes*, p. 34.

7 Bantum, Brian, "The Church Cannot be About Multiculturalism," video by Quest Church (December 1, 2009) https://vimeo.com/7912443.

8 Bantum, Gail Song and Brian Bantum, *Choosing Us: Marriage and Mutual Flourishing in a World of Difference* (Brazos Press, 2022).

9 Thurman, Howard, *Jesus and the Disinherited* (Beacon Press, 1976), p.6–8.

CHAPTER 7

1 Jennings, Willie James, *Belief, A Theological Commentary on the Bible: Acts* (Westminister John Knox, 2017), p. 39–40.

CHAPTER 8

1 Augustine, *The City of God Against the Pagans*, Vol. 2, Loeb Classical Library, trans. William McAllen Green (Cambridge, MA: Harvard University Press, 1963), p. 465 (section 7.24); Megan DeFranza, "Virtuous Eunuchs: Troubling Conservative and Queer Readings of Intersex and the Bible," chapter 2 in *Intersex, Theology, and the Bible Troubling Bodies in Church, Text, and Society*, ed. Susannah Cornwall (Palgrave Macmillan, 2016), p.58.

CHAPTER 9

1 Barclay, John, *Paul and the Power of Grace* (Eerdmans, 2020), p. 1.

2 Edwards, Jonathan, "Sinners in the Hands of an Angry God." A sermon preached at Enfield, July 8, 1741, https://digitalcommons .unl.edu/cgi/viewcontent.cgi?article=1053&context=etas.

3 Cortina, Matthew, "Mark Driscoll Sermons: Tells Mars Hill Congregation 'God Hates Some of You' (VIDEO)" *The Christian Post* (October 9, 2011), https://www.christianpost.com/news/mark -driscoll-at-catalyst-atlanta-fear-not-dad-is-with-us.html.

4 Bonhoeffer, Dietrich, *Discipleship: Dietrich Bonhoeffer Works—Reader's Edition (Fortress Press, 2015), p. 5.*

NOTES

CHAPTER 10

1 Credit to Morgan Guyton for the insight that many modern translations miss the meaning: that God is choosing people, not "things".

2 Brown, Brené, *Braving the Wilderness: The Quest for True Belonging and the Courage to Stand Alone* (Random House, 2019), p. x.

3 Peter Vogt, ed., *Our Moravian Treasures: A Manual of Topics for Theological Education in the Unitas Fratrum* (Worldwide Moravian Church Unity Office, Christiansfeld, Denmark, 2019), p.59–63.

CHAPTER 11

1 "Looking at Bothsidesing: When Equal Coverage Leads to Uneven Results," *Merriam-Webster*, https://www.merriam-webster.com/words-at-play/bothsidesing-bothsidesism-new-words-were-watching.

2 Rashid, Jonny, *Jesus Takes a Side: Embracing the Political Demands of the Gospel* (Herald Press, 2022), p. 50.

3 Cornel West, *Twitter* February 14, 2017, https://twitter.com/CornelWest/status/831718432995319808?s=20.